Lucid Death

Lucid Death

Conscious Journeys Beyond the Threshold

KIENDA BETRUE

WITH A FOREWORD BY NANCY JEWEL POER

iUniverse, Inc.
Bloomington

Lucid Death
Conscious Journeys Beyond the Threshold

iUniverse books may be ordered through booksellers or by contacting:

iUniverse
1663 Liberty Drive
Bloomington, IN 47403
www.iuniverse.com
1-800-Authors (1-800-288-4677)

ISBN: 978-1-4620-6117-4 (sc)
ISBN: 978-1-4620-6118-1 (ebk)

Printed in the United States of America

iUniverse rev. date: 08/28/2012

This book is dedicated to the ones I love,
including you, Gentle Reader.

"All hastening onward, yet none seemed to know whither he went, or whence he came, or why."

Percy Bysshe Shelly from *The Triumph of Life*

FOREWORD BY NANCY JEWEL POER

Books like this one, which take seriously the relationship between those living and working on the planet and those in spiritual worlds, are welcome and needed. The knowledge of karma and reincarnation is essential if we are to have an awakened humanity. We must become fully aware of the justice of karma; the universal law of cause and effect. Then we can be motivated to moral deeds for the world. Sufficient numbers of people are needed to take on the greater mission of working toward the positive evolution of our future world: a world we are challenged to create with the help, guidance and inspiration of the cosmic leaders of the universe, as this book urges. But in this age of the consciousness soul and freedom, the spiritual worlds wait for us to take up this task, out of free choice – our free will.

I cannot speak from direct experience of Kienda's insights and therapeutic work, but the rich and poignant descriptions of many lives, deaths, and reincarnations are certainly compelling. One can readily recognize that she came into this life with gifts of clairvoyance from childhood, which she has worked to ground with spiritual study. It is clear that she has dedicated her work and gifts to helping others. In the therapeutic approach she takes, not only is great integrity essential in the therapist, but the freedom of the individual clients involved is paramount for unfolding the healing wisdom they need to walk their life path in fuller consciousness. This is important work for our time

Kienda and I both share the universal, all-encompassing world view of Anthroposophy (wisdom of humanity). Anthroposophy is the fruit of the extraordinary insights of Rudolf Steiner, the twentieth-century seer whose work has inspired culturally healing endeavors to transform every aspect of life: education, arts, agriculture, architecture, medicine, and more. From this world view, Kienda has quite ably endeavored to synthesize the basic principles of life on earth and life in cosmic existence, and to illuminate the fact that death is simply a journey into the realms that surround us unseen while we are living. The book's vivid descriptive pictures give a glimpse into experiences between lives; into levels of learning and awakening there, and into the tasks of karmic working groups in the spiritual world. Through the stories, she shows the relationship of death and the afterlife in different religions and epochs of history; the truth of evolving consciousness of the soul; and places the deed of Christ as the central event on the earth. The goal of learning to experience Cosmic Love is at the heart of humanity's destiny, for as she states, "Christ is not just a religious figure, but a cosmic force of evolution."

As a national home death consultant, I work with threshold groups and individuals to strengthen and support their loved ones in the spiritual world. Kienda and I, each in our own way, are both deeply committed to strengthening the healthy bonds between the living and the so-called dead. As we are living in one of the most challenging and decisive times for the future of humanity, we have never needed this partnership more. Those in spirit have the big picture and can inspire and inform those of us working here. We can do what they can only hope for. The actual deeds for changing the world can be done only here on earth.

Nancy Jewel Poer, Michaelmas, 2011

Nancy Jewel Poer is a nationally recognized pioneer and consultant in the home death movement. Her seminal book, *Living Into Dying, Spiritual and Practical Deathcare for Family and Community* has empowered many families to care for their own loved ones at death. In 2010 she directed and produced *The Most Excellent Dying of Theodore Jack Heckelman,* a documentary film on conscious dying that has won two national awards. She also has published a book for children dealing with loss, *The Tear, A Children's Story of Hope and Transformation When a Loved One Dies.*

Available on her website www. nancyjewelpoer.com

ACKNOWLEDGMENTS

First, I offer profound gratitude for the physical and spiritual assistance that has been gifted to me. Next, I lovingly acknowledge my three daughters, Mariko, D'aria Rose, and Athena—three dynamic, talented, wise, and compassionate individuals. I thank my son, Christian Alexander, who from the spiritual worlds since his SIDS death more than thirty years ago, has met me at the threshold and pulled aside the veil, allowing me glimpses beyond.

My whole family is a loving support system, and I express my deep love and gratitude to all: my sainted mother, Bunny, my father, Curtiss, and Frank, my sisters Ariel and Janet, my brothers Curt and Doug and his beautiful wife Lisa, and to all the gaggle of nieces and nephews, in-laws, aunts, uncles, cousins, and all my relations.

To Ignacio Cisneros, I offer my thanks for having "seen" me. Recognition soul to soul is an affirming, empowering experience. Such joy I wish to everyone.

Thanks for the cover art goes to Ignacio Cisneros and Aaron Quick, two patient, gifted artists.

To my dear friend Mary Rubach, I offer appreciation and gratitude for her financial and spiritual support.

Rudolf Steiner has my undying gratitude and respect for having shown the way to experience spiritual realities. Thank you Dr. Steiner. It really works.

Since this book began as a master's thesis, I thank everyone who took part in that laborious process. The book has been only a slightly easier affair.

And to everyone I have ever known or encountered, whether in person; through your writings, music or performances; in dreams or visions; for good or bad; whatever the case may have been, I thank you for the opportunities our interactions have afforded and the growth and insight our meetings have fostered. So, I guess that ultimately, I should just thank Prime Creator, and everyone in the world, the galaxy, and the universe. And I do.

TABLE OF CONTENTS

INTRODUCTION

Life and Death are two sides of the same coin, two halves of the full circle of existence. But we who are alive at this moment can only see one side, one half. What do we know about the shadow of life—death? Our normal five senses only observe the animate, physically alive side. How can we know the other?

From time immemorial, there have been ways and means of garnering impressions from sleep and the spiritual worlds, which is also where death resides. These worlds are imperceptible to the senses and ordinary conscious thought. However, when the ability to see into the spiritual worlds is awakened and disciplined, and our mental processes expand beyond material limitations and focus on the dimensions beyond the perceptible vibratory range of the five senses, incredibly vast arenas of existence and experience open up.

The secret mystery schools of the past and the various initiations into priesthood stimulated the perceptive organs of the soul of the candidates, so that in dreams and vision quests, neophytes could experience spiritual realms, and understand their inherent meaning and relationship to human, earth-bound life. The practices that awakened the subtle organs of spiritual perception were based on an esoteric understanding of the nature and constitution of the human being, which include faculties, organs, and energy fields beyond the mere physical body; these are the etheric, astral, and spiritual Ego/I. These integral, though invisible, parts of every person are what leave the body at death and move out into the unseen realms of their origin. There they are resolved within the parameters of their native realm, dimension or vibratory range, just as the material body remains on earth and eventually returns to the constituent elements of the physical plane such as carbon, oxygen, nitrogen and iron.

In our day and age, 2000-something AD, humanity as a whole has evolved the possibility of perceiving spiritual realms. Meditation, the near-death experience (NDE), fasting, yoga, breathing techniques, and mental activities such as sacred geometry, are a few of the practices, activities, and experiences available now that exercise the subtle fields and awaken the functioning of the inner organs of perception. These organs are the third eye or spiritual pineal, the preceptor of imaginative insight or clairvoyance; the inner ear of inspiration or clairaudience; the spiritual pituitary of inner knowing, intuition or clairsentience; and the spiritual heart, the generator and chalice of love, our truest human quality.

With these awakened organs, one can perceive the spiritual motivation behind the worldly state of being and activity, both in nature and the human being. These are the faculties that expedite self-realization and self-actualization. Of course, in the meantime, all through and in between, we are simply and compassionately and absolutely human, which means that we are fine, wonderful and successful. But we also fail and "blow it," and live messy human lives fraught with hope and despair, illusion and cold reality, love and hate; that is, every duality, which we must learn to balance. The biggest duality to realize and balance is life and death. So this is a book about that very thing: learning to embrace consciously the light *and* the shadow—Life and Death.

A bit of a personal confession is appropriate at the beginning. As a child, I saw fairies, gnomes, ghosts, and angels, and it hasn't stopped. Not all the time, mind you; but it still happens in moments of greatest delight, profoundest sorrow, or deepest meditation. I am grateful for these glimpses beyond the veil of outer appearances. They have come as the fruit of disciplined inner work and as gifts of grace. From them I have gained a sense of solidity, a feeling of security, in that I know through my own experience from an early age, that there is more than meets the physical senses. I don't just hope or wish; I know!

I have recently come to realize that "I" am the thread that ties the varied parts of my lives and experiences together. At first, I tried to remove myself from this book and let the stories and experiences speak for themselves, but it felt incomplete. Having gone through the academic system, I had been impressed with the idea that I had to remove myself from my work to be accurate, accepted, and taken seriously. This troubled me. There is something in academic bias that does not apply to life itself, to art, or experiences in the spiritual world. In non-academic social circles, I had to distance myself from my experiences, or appear conceited and selfish. I trust I have found the balance in this book. My consciousness and clear thinking are the ties that bind it all together into a comprehensible whole.

After writing my academic master's thesis, I edited it for book publication and cut out almost everything but the stories. I have now matured through the grace of time, and with a little help from my friends, I have come to realize the validity of my own authorship, and the duties there of. I must and do claim my experiences and honor my process. It is not only the information about life after death that is important. The methods for exploring these worlds are also valuable. The tools by which one perceives the spiritual worlds are publicly available and by my example, prove effective when practiced diligently and with moral fortitude

(an old fashioned term, but still current in the spiritual worlds.)

Human consciousness is evolving toward greater, more profound interaction with spiritual beings of other hierarchies and dimensions. We humans have tasks awaiting our arrival and participation in the multitudinous planes of our earthly, solar, and galactic environments. In this book are some of my other-worldly adventures and the path my friends and I have taken. We bushwhacked our way into the spiritual world and then found vast cities, realms, and worlds already there and flourishing. We followed some known trails and some time-honored exercises and practices, like meditation and yoga, and the indications of Rudolf Steiner. I created my own meditative practices and did them rigorously through all kinds of metamorphoses over decades. Each step on this self-chosen (and sometimes self-created), path brought me to higher places and broader vantage points.

Various workshops and trainings from contemporary seekers and finders added to my spiritual tool box: Inter-dimensional Consciousness Training and Sound Healing with Tom Kenyon, Alchemical Hypnotherapy Certification by David Quigley, Reiki, Tai Chi, and Emotional Freedom Technique (EFT), to name only a few. I subsequently chose bits and pieces from nearly every one as they fit my personal needs on my own individual path. There is no "one size fits all" spirituality. Only we, ourselves, guided by our own specific guardian angel, and our own discerning, pure, sense-free thinking can find the most appropriate access and connection to the spiritual worlds and the diverse beings who reside there.

A word of cautious consideration is perhaps appropriate here. The spiritual worlds all have laws and conditions that are very different from physically based, earth life. It is advisable to be informed. From time immemorial, the knowledge of the cosmic truths underlying the spiritual worlds has been revealed to humanity in visions and teachings appropriate to the age and stage of human development. There are time-honored principles which form a grounding anchor-point and guide for discernment when crossing the threshold into the spiritual worlds, such as: goodness, beauty, and truth; nobility, compassion, and morality.

I personally am steeped in the world view of Anthroposophy (or Spiritual Science) as expressed by Rudolf Steiner. His methods of clear thinking clairvoyance, clairaudience, and clairsentience are the blossoming in modern times of the wisdom of the western occult traditions; from Plato, Aristotle, the Rosicrucians, and Theosophists into Anthroposophy, the divine wisdom of humankind.

From many years of patient study and practice, I have developed an intelligent, balanced basis for conscious journeys into the spiritual worlds which seems to work in the twenty-first century. From my perspective, humanity needs to journey beyond the threshold, now. Now is the time. Future frontiers are not only on distant stars, but also deep within the human soul. In an encouraging spirit of good will and support, I offer this book *Lucid Death, Conscious Journeys Beyond the Threshold.* May it enrich your life, and guide you through your adventures in death's domain.

The hypnotherapy journeys (also referred to as spiritual regressions) that I facilitated and those I experienced myself are further glimpses into the other worlds. These journeys are best described as gently facilitated inner explorations, with the client/subject in a profoundly relaxed yet conscious state. As time is immaterial, especially in the spiritual worlds where space is immaterial as well, verb tenses sometimes shift about. Logical sequential time is often presented simultaneously or instantaneously. An earthly human being is challenged to express these amazing and often non-verbal states and experiences in normal language. I shall refer to the client/subject of the sessions in this book as the "traveler," since that person is journeying in other dimensions to retrieve memories of past lives, deaths, and rebirths.

Spiritual Regression: *Pre-Earthly Experience of the Author*

I include a personal journey here as explanation for my interest and involvement in this work, which explores the journey of the soul between death and rebirth.

I went into the heaven world, just before this lifetime, and there I was, a little disheveled angel child with bare feet. I was arguing with three large luminous beings. "I don't want to go down to earth again—at least not so soon. That last short life and that hideous death in Auschwitz was toooo traumatic. I am NOT ready for another life! I want to stay here in the warm baths!! I wanna heal some more!!! I DON'T WANNA GO!!!!" But the big angels just shake their heads sweetly and say that there is a wonderful opportunity waiting for me—the perfect parents who are gentle and kind, and it really is a good time. If I stay here and heal, then I will not have the "properties" or the right constitution to do what I need to do.

So I say, "Okay, what is it that I need to do in this next lifetime that's so darned important that it just can't wait?" The angels lovingly gather me up in their collective arms of compassion and take me to a room to see a living movie on a living screen about all the many exciting possibilities for the next life. When it is finished, I know that what I need to do next time is: *remember through everything,* and that my job will be to *bring other worlds through into this next life coming up.* I am still feeling raw from that dreadful last life, but waiting and healing aren't right, because

I won't be able to remember through everything if I am all healed up; and I won't be able to even see the other worlds, much less do anything about them, unless I have some broken and unhealed places in myself.

I wasn't too crazy about the idea of hanging on to my broken spots, much less getting any new ones, but the scenario didn't look too bad, really. I would need some minor childhood trauma; not violent abuse, like last time, but just my dear Grandmother's instability—she wandered between the worlds but couldn't handle it. When she came on the screen, she was so sad and sweet, and wounded herself, that I loved her anyway. I was so damaged already, that even gentle trauma would keep me open. I wouldn't fit together perfectly and seamlessly like normal people, so there would be cracks between the worlds. If I were to have a perfectly lovely childhood, I might get complacent—I would, in all probability, forget. So Grandma agreed to play this part in my life—to help keep me off balance so I can remember, and see the other worlds, and tell the truth. My Mom and Dad-to-be are there too. They were chosen and agreed because they are good, open-hearted, spiritual people. They won't need to patch up the cracks. They are pretty stable, centered souls who aren't afraid for themselves, and so they will allow me to be the way that I am, or will be, or at least could be. Anyway, they won't try to "fix" me.

By the time the movie was over, I got it—the big picture, I mean. I still didn't feel ready, but it's hard to argue with big angels and win, and besides the whole plan made perfect sense. So I agreed.

This book is one of the results.

CHAPTER 1

Setting the Stage

The questions, "Why am I born?" and "Why am I living?" have passed through every human being's mind at some point in their lives, perhaps incessantly. And of course, the corollary is, "Since I am here for whatever reason, then why must I die?" It is usually only innocent children, existentially driven artists, and mad poets who verbalize these questions and confront the issues in a public setting; however, doubt and the desire to know are resident within all human hearts.

Historically, religions have addressed these questions. They have shepherded their believers through the events of life and death, with each religion having arisen from within a particular culture at a particular time in history and world evolution. The different religious doctrines answered the questions that humanity was asking, which were appropriate to the stage of development of the majority of the people living in a particular time and place. But where are we now? What stage has humanity achieved? What are the faculties and capacities we possess, as a whole and as individuals, and what questions are we asking? In other words, what are we ready to discover and know?

In my observation, I sense that humanity is asking to know and experience the meaning of existence, the heights and depths of it, which must include not only bright life itself, but also its shadow: death. To the degree that we can each individually focus our consciousness, we are awake, aware, and thinking in our daily lives. But sleep and death are in the shadowland of the unconscious. Science has dissected life and matter down to atoms, quarks, and quantum strings, but we know very little about the subconscious and superconscious realms, those dimensions below and above what can be weighed and measured. These are the largely uncharted landscapes of the so-called "spiritual worlds," and sleep and death are doorways into them. Humanity is now poised to explore this last frontier.

Since the Renaissance, philosophy, rationalism, and materialism have eroded the faith-based acceptance of dogmatic answers to these deepest queries into the meaning of life, death, birth, and infinity. The scientific and industrial revolutions have severed humanity from the embrace of nature, and driven the wedge deeper in the schism between the physical and the spiritual; what we see and the meaning behind it. In our lifetime, the questioning is becoming strident, as the earth is being polluted, childhood has become a battleground, and illness and plagues are ravaging earth's population. We humans have had millennia to pursue our answers, and repeated earth lives to polish up the lessons. We have had multiple opportunities, spread over time and across the face of the globe, to awaken, remember, cognize, and know. And although most religions still offer possible scenarios for the meaning of existence and the experiences after death, they are not satisfying the intelligent contemporary seeker, much less the few spiritually perceptive observers.

In the fields of Lucid Dreaming and Tibetan Dream Yoga, the goal is to achieve a state of conscious awareness and participation in events during sleep. In Lucid Death, the goal is to consciously participate in the journey of the soul through dying, death, and into whatever lies beyond. This means the ultimate integration of all polarities: light and dark; conscious and unconscious; life and death. The premise of Jungian psychology that the shadow side of an individual must be integrated for health and wholeness, rings true. Since death is our darkest shadow, we must meet, explore, and embrace it.

In every culture and throughout history, there have always been a few brave or unwitting souls who have journeyed beyond Death's door. Their archetypal stories have been the impetus for the world's great religions and cults. The travelers themselves often became high priests and shamans, revered and respected for the wisdom and guidance they brought back from "the other side." Consider Buddha's enlightenment under the Bo tree, which culminated in his vanquishing Yama, Lord of Death, who was in the form of Mara, the Evil one; and Christ's descent into Hell, releasing the souls trapped in death on Holy Saturday, before the Easter Resurrection. The Egyptian god Osiris endured two deaths and resurrections before himself becoming the Lord of the Underworld. Inanna of Babylon descended into the realm of Erishkagil, Queen of Death, to retrieve Dumuzi, her lost husband. Greek Demeter's persistence brought her daughter Persephone back to earth from the dead for half of the year, assuring life's continuation with spring and summer. Most religions and cults celebrate the overcoming of death through rebirth because those are the forces with which we will all reckon in our own times.

What the world religions have described beyond death has shaped human belief, and belief is a force that affects the quality of life. Belief is the bedrock of world view, ethics and morality. It is a powerful force in life, and may affect the afterlife as well. There are similarities among the many belief systems, philosophies, and religions; but the differences, especially about what happens after death, are far more dramatic, ranging from elaborate afterworlds and cosmic plans, on the one hand, to complete annihilation and the void on the other; and of course, everything in between.

How can this vast, amorphous historical body of knowledge and belief be understood today? What is the journey of the contemporary soul? And further, of what possible use could such knowledge be? To answer the last question first, just imagine that *what you think happens after death, does happen.* Were this so, it would behoove us individually and collectively to consider death and beyond. When life and death are seen as the complete circle that they are, then growth and learning and evolution never stop and what we do here affects there, and vice versa. It is time to integrate death consciously into our waking life. It is time to embrace lucid death.

This book is a recreation of my master's thesis. In the scholarly piece, I viewed death and the journey thereafter from many points of view: the near-death experience (NDE); hospice; sudden infant death syndrome (SIDS); the anatomy and physiology of dying and death; Lucid Dreaming; Tibetan dream yoga; philosophy; and religion. These were all fascinating aspects, and each yielded invaluable facts and facets of the changing face of death.

Since the material gathered here first appeared as a master's thesis, my gentle readers can rest assured that every possible quote and paraphrase was correctly cited and footnoted in the original. In the twelve years since then, however, the material has gestated in my mind and soul, and the book is my own version of the perennial cosmology. In the extensive bibliography, the most salient books are starred (*), and the books from which direct quotes of any length are taken, are double starred (**).

As a clinical hypnotherapist, I created a protocol to explore a past life, the journey beyond death, and the succeeding incarnation. My facilitation style is usually very carefully non-suggestive, asking only, "and then what happens?" or "what do you notice now?" in order to allow the greatest freedom for the traveler's individual perceptions and experiences. The crux of my work is to be found in these spiritual regression hypnotherapy journeys, as well as the western esoteric world model which includes life and death, and karma, transformation, and reincarnation, in the cosmic scheme.

The work of Rudolf Steiner, spiritual scientist, explains in logical concepts the unfolding of karma and reincarnation, and the journey after death. This information is of inestimable value for the modern mind that wants to know "why" and "how," "where" and "when." It provides a conceptual matrix based on the evolution of consciousness, in which to place all the information and experiences about the journey of the soul between death and rebirth, as well as in everyday life. A comprehensive cognitive womb or conceptual matrix is indispensable in our day and age. Life is a puzzle, and we all have pieces to offer. Humanity needs a big picture to organize all the pieces.

Neither earth life nor the spiritual world is a willy-nilly free-for-all. Contrary to certain ideas popular in the wishful-thinking New Age, we do not conjure up existence through our intentions and affirmations. Yes, thoughts and feelings have effects; but there is an objective spiritual reality, just as there is an objective physical reality, although the two are very different. Learning about the spiritual worlds and vast cosmic ages is one thing. Experiencing them is another. An open, receptive, but discerning mind is the first step to coherent spiritual experiences. Clear, focused, intelligent, logical, discriminating thinking applied to those experiences is the next step. A compassionate heart is yet another key to accurate spiritual perception.

The earlier religions arose as the evolutionary need arose. Then, having fulfilled their purpose, they subsided back into cultural history. The major religions that have continued into the present have changed, modified and adapted to the needs of succeeding ages, with varying degrees of success and beneficence. Some, such as Hinduism and Confucianism, continue primarily within their original cultural streams. Others, such as Buddhism and Christianity, spread beyond their cultural roots to become global religious movements. Although each religion contains specific dogma of the afterlife, in my limited experience, Tibetan Buddhism and Esoteric Christianity have expressed their views the most clearly and comprehensibly.

The chapters on these two religions and world views will be expanded and elaborated to create a conceptual matrix within which to better understand the journey of the soul between death and rebirth, from eastern and western points of view. The information for the journey of the soul after death in Chapter 5 – Buddhism, comes from translations of the *Tibetan Book of the Dead* by Francesca Freemantle and Chogyam Trungpa; by Robert Thurmond; by Lati Rinpoche and Jeffry Hopkins; and from Sogyal Rinpoche's *The Tibetan Book of Living and Dying*. These books are indicated by a (#) in the bibliography. The basis for Chapter 8 – Esoteric Christianity is found in many of the lecture cycles and books by Rudolf Steiner. Other anthroposophical authors give vivid descriptions of the journey of the soul between death and rebirth, especially Stanley Drake, in his book *Though You Die: Death and Life Beyond Death*.

The other chapters contain a brief paragraph or two about a specific religion and have all been inspired by Houston Smith's beautiful book, *The Illustrated World Religions: A Guide to our Wisdom Traditions*. A verbatim transcript of a spiritual regression hypnotherapy session follows each description. They are in a **san serif font** to differentiate them from the expository text (which you are now reading.) After the transcript, there is a paragraph or two underscoring important aspects of the journey.

The spiritual regression stories are individual human experiences that illustrate cultural and religious beliefs, as the travelers use their own words and concepts to identify objects and experiences in the spiritual worlds. They represent the human side of the cosmic drama. The head (theory) and heart (experience) are telling the same story; macrocosm and microcosm. And you, Gentle Reader, must supply the will to understand it all, and perhaps adjust your life accordingly; if not here, then, certainly on the other side. May the information contained here serve you well in life and in death.

Chapter 2

Primitive Cultures

In the ancient mists of time, original, primal beliefs were associated with the native geography, flora, and fauna. Because they began long before history was recorded, the stories based on the relationships of people and their environments were passed orally from generation to generation: from grandfather to father to son to grandson, and from grandmother to mother to daughter to granddaughter, and on and on. The primal worldview is all-inclusive: all life is cradled in a cosmic womb. Everything is alive. It is a visionary world of animism, where time is eternal, space is actual in soil, stone, tree, and stream, and human memory holds the threads of past, present, and future. The boundary between mythological and physically actual is indistinct and unimportant, since all life in the primeval beginnings of mankind and the world is fresh from the hands of the creator. The primal creation stories often link the beginning with the end; the creation of life, with death.

Spiritual Regression: Nnanndi a Pygmy and Pheidalon from Thrace

The following verbatim story, transcribed from notes taken during the session, illustrates the flow of life and death as experienced in a primitive culture, set in the jungles of central Africa. The traveler, KM, is a storyteller herself, a sculptor, and a former Waldorf teacher. She speaks several languages and her education is rich in mythology and ancient history. This story, told under the light trance of hypnotherapy, is mystical in mood and poetic in its language, appropriate for the time before the development of the conceptual intellect, in harmony with the natural setting, and fitting for the ancient beginnings of human life.

(The induction was a deep body relaxation (An induction is an individually tailored protocol to relax the traveler, intended to facilitate serenity and deep introspection. The will of the facilitator is never applied, thus leaving the traveler completely free.) *The client's associative stream of conscious brought her immediately into the inner ear, which became a cave.)*

People and animals are in this cave, with tunnels like the cochlea and the fluid in it all working perfectly. It is the portal of listening. I am a flow of water through the chambers of the earth. It is the headwaters, cool and quiet and dark, which run down silently into a pool: a spring. I see the opening and it's dark in there. I am supposed to go inside. Very tiny little "somethings" live here. They are little simple cave creatures, blind fish and other creatures, and they are all very small. It is the beginning of the evolution of animals, the differentiation of land and sea creatures.

(I suggested that KM might ask a question of the little animals if she wanted to, but she answered . . .)

It is not a place for asking questions: it is a place for sentience with the body. It is the gate of birth for generations. It's like being in an organ inside the body; larynx, fallopian tube, any and all. I have come down here to learn to listen: it is shaped much like the ear. When the ear listens, it's still. You can't hear when you are moving. Mold and fungus and algae are there in the cave/ear and sentient. I look at a moss growing on a rock; it looks like a jungle up close. This bit of green slime is a whole world teeming with life like a tropical jungle. It's like the earth from space. It's just a smear until you get close, then I hear the voices of all the beings going on at once, almost like a nebula. Next to it (the smear of algae growing on a rock) is a black hole created in a stone with water coming out of it. This is the hole to the center of the earth that the Navaho speak of, the Sipapu. Stones are made of the universe, not vice versa. This little green scrap is singing the song of life; a celestial chorus.

(I suggested gently that she move on to her past life.)

(Past Life) Now the sound is like pygmies singing in the forest and they sing as they gather—spontaneous, long songs about each other in four and six parts. They sing as they work because working makes you sing. I am a little woman. I look like a grandmother but my own baby is on my hip so I have two hands free and I am gathering leaves and roots and bark and putting them in a basket. I am digging roots. I am singing about another who did silly things and I'm teasing. We speak a tonal language. We are creatures of the forest, so deep and silent. The canopy is so high, but we never get lost. I speak the language of the moss and animals. I can't fly but the birds do and I can ask them about it. The other women gather food, but I gather herbs; the plants speak to me in smell and taste.

I go back to the village of little transient huts of vines and leaves. We go in at night; it keeps the chill and rain off, and keeps animals out. Each woman has a hut. Life is a river, but we avoid the big river, the Congo, it's a break in the canopy and we don't like it, we are of the forest. *(The juxtaposition of the contemporary name of Africa's Congo River into this ancient journey is just one of the many anachronisms that may appear in these circumstances.)*

In the village I have a little fire and cook in the ashes on a spit. Children are playing: they have no clothing. The men are singing as they come back with game. There is a singing and response between the men and the women and children in the village.

(KM was speaking very slowly and so I asked, "Is there anything else to see here?" and she stopped and then continued.)

I am Nnanndi. I have a child of three or four; I had others but they have died or gone away. *(I suggested that she move forward to the next important event in Nnanndi's life and she went immediately to her death.)*

(Death) I am an old woman knowing that death is coming and I sing my song and the songs of the universe and creation and the origin of creatures and my people and my family and my birth—the song that welcomed me, that the village sang at my birth and all the songs of childhood, puberty and the songs of work. I sing all the songs of my life. I am alone beside my hut. We are nomadic people and all the others have left. I sent my people on ahead because I will migrate to a different place: that is the way of my people. I stayed here, to sing my great sweet song of the world and my place in it. And now I sing my death song because I know it's time to go. After my songs and preparations I lie in the doorway of my hut and give up my soul. *(There was a very brief pause, and as I prepared to suggest forward movement, KM took a deep breath and continued.)*

(After Death) As I leave my body, there is a great shout from the periphery, a shout of joy. I step into the light and begin a forgetting of who I was, like a sunrise. The facets of my being were held by wax and the warmth of the light melts the wax and it loses its form and the porous bony inner nature, my identity, crumbles. The waxy substance drains away, like amber tree sap and burns off in the sunshine and all flows together and cools to the consistency of quicksilver, but of a beautiful golden color. Eventually, it comes out of the hole at the bottom of the cave as water. Nnanndi dissolves and comes through the water and the

golden sap. It is cool and dark in the waters and in the tradition of my people, we lean back into it and listen to a memory of golden light, and only then do we say "I remember" to the light; and then the tide turns and the waters flow in the other direction. When we emerge from the hole in the earth, we are in the darkness and we emerge from the darkness as from sleep. We open our eyes and see only the reflected light; the Sun is at our backs. We go out into the world before dawn and see the colors and always welcome the Sun, but the Sun is only the moon to the spiritual light.

(I asked if Nnanndi's song became a part of the oral tradition of her people, and KM replied.) The children coming forth do not remember my song, because it is not important. They look forward not back: their faces are turned to the Sun. Salmon don't look back when they want to go to the sea, only when they reach the sea, for then the source becomes the goal.

(KM had come to a stop again, and I suggested that she move forward to the next important experience.)

(Reincarnation) Nnanndi emerges as a little boy, mischievous, laughing, mercurial, and growing quickly. He is a miracle baby who grows so fast. Then comes playing war and marching; playing king and leader in battle. He is a very intelligent youth but of an unpredictable nature, playing at conquest like Alexander the Great. He has qualities like Alexander (memory and a ferocious determination) and he is skilled at many things. He is a young nobleman, in a cohort of Alexander's companions, a general who is assigned to hold Alexandria as a place for learning.

Part of him knows that Nnanndi is his real spiritual mother, so the women who love him are not of real importance to him. He treats them as a man would a concubine; he pleases and is kind, but with no deep interest or respect. He does not respect his own father, either. One reason he is a fine warrior is because he knows what she (Nnanndi) knows about Death.

21

His name is Pheidalon, and he comes from Thrace on the edge of the Black Sea. It is Hellenistic times. He is arrogant and overconfident and domineering, the kind of man who doesn't see inferiors or peasants as being human or like himself. However, he is deeply admired by men, being charismatic, beautiful to look upon, and skilled in weapons and tools. And he wins contests. The world is full of contests and he is good at winning. He has the qualities of silver and black. He is considered cold or distant because his real spiritual companion is Nnanndi. She appears at night to him when he prays. She is the only one he really listens to.

Nnanndi sings to him, "My son is a beautiful stag and king of the herd, and he is the one the hunters will want to pursue and one day bring down. His heavy rack grows heavier with more points as he conquers all. But one day he will be caught and brought down. The does work and sing together; the stag lives alone. And the men will carry him home singing in response with the women about the courage and nobility of the stag who defended his territory until he met the stag's death. The king must die the Stag's Death." *(Here the lives and deaths of the two incarnations have become entwined and the metaphors blend.)*

(Death) The stag's death is not a difficult death. A blow loosens the consciousness from the body and the soul is free to go. As Pheidalon crosses over into the light, Nnanndi is waiting for him and says, "Welcome, my son. You have done well." He smiles the smile of the victor who has received the highest honor and prize. He died young, at thirty or thirty-two, having gone out into the world. The stag is the king of the forest and Nnanndi was the mother of the king of the forest.

In ancient cultures and primitive societies still living in harmony with nature; life and death have always been as simple and natural as waking and sleeping. Time and the rhythms of life were set by the Sun and Moon, and co-operative community relationships among the people mirrored the harmony and interdependence of their environment. Days were concluded as the Sun went down and the people slept in their beds. Life was concluded at death and the people slept in the earth. Death was just a longer, deeper sleep. In this journey, the flow from one life to another life is metaphorically just a stream of golden light and water.

Nnanndi concluded her own life as she sang her *kamaloca* (Sanskrit for "place of desire"—the astral plane where the emotions of life are relived and balanced.) This she did before crossing the threshold into death. She inscribed all her life memories in song, sound, and rhythm, and created her own life tableau. By doing so, she had no necessity for "purgatorial" experience, and the afterlife was an easy flow. She had already remembered, resolved, and honored the events of her life to her last moments.

In those ancient times, prayer to the ancestors created a close spiritual bond which kept the channels of communication open between the living and the dead, between one incarnation and the next, between Nnanndi and Pheidalon.

CHAPTER 3

Hinduism

The Hindu religion is one of the oldest recorded on earth; the myths and legends emerging from prehistoric depths. In ancient times of human evolution, when the Hindu religion and culture were firmly established, the gods referred to were not the supreme creators of the universe, but rather centers of spiritual intelligence, and beings of lesser hierarchies that co-evolved with the human race. All of the cosmos is evolving, including the gods and *devas*. Each succeeding earthly civilization with its attendant hierarchy of guiding spiritual beings, depicts a stage in the evolution of consciousness clothed in the appropriate cultural values and styles of the time.

In Hinduism, human life is understood as evolving through innumerable incarnations driven to ever-higher states of consciousness by the law of karma, which is basically that you reap what you sow; in the next lifetime, if not in this one.

Spiritual Regression: *Nataranja in Ancient India and Gangaji, also in Ancient India*

Two related sessions of the author's were spent exploring ancient Indian incarnations. They revealed the following story and the cosmic overview as well. A very brief description of the end of the life is all that came from the session because I had become aware of this past life twenty or more years prior to the hypnotherapy sessions. The whole lifetime as Nataranja had opened up in my consciousness as I embraced a young naturopath in farewell, after a conference in which we both participated. It was an intense experience and heralded the time in my present life when I began the study of eurythmy, a form of spiritual movement.

When I was researching my thesis, some twenty or more years later, I returned to the Nataranja lifetime and followed her into the spiritual worlds beyond death, which had not been a part of my former experience. The end of the life, the death, the after-death experiences and the next incarnation are included, illustrating that the circumstances and beliefs of life influence the world of death, and that the lessons learned in death influence the next life.

(The induction included a little boat with a ferryman sitting in the back, poling our barque upstream into the past. I had brought a pillow to lean against, to better trail my hand in the warm water. The scenes on the shore blurred, though we were really moving very slowly. Both banks were glazed in dreamy light until up ahead I could see a dark sky and a fire on the bank.)

(Past Life) Tabla and other drums were pattering frenzied rhythms into the tropical night as we reached the shore and I stepped out of the boat, a haggard, gray-haired, toothless old woman, holding my ragged sari to hide my worn out body. I wasn't old, really, but life had been hard since I had been driven from my husband's house for a mere flirtation with the young Brahmin scholar. It was easy to become a destitute caste-less woman in the sprawling, writhing city on the banks of Mother Ganga, and it was all that was left for me until the hill thieves took me in. But when all that ended in bloodshed and sorrow, I aged quickly, and now I found myself washed up on the shore, huddled around the

garbage fire, watching the gleaming firelight and shadows play over the faces of my nameless fellow derelicts making music in the perfumed night. A young woman begins to dance, and soon two or three others join her.

So very long ago, I trained as a temple dancer. So very long ago the dance was my joy and my life, but marriage to the fat merchant stopped that. Dancing for him was disgusting, salacious, no longer pure, or a pathway to divine knowing. And since the day my robber love was so brutally killed, dancing did not exist for me. But tonight is different. I can almost feel my lover's arms around me. I hear temple bells ringing in my ears and the tabla pulls my feet into movement. Oh, God, oh, Goddess, I am dancing. An old bag of bones whirling and stamping, dipping and swaying, oblivious to all but the music. In frenzied ecstasy, I dance my life and death; everything I have suffered and enjoyed, all my hopes, dreams, and despair. When the dance is finished, so am I. To the applause and appreciation of the motley circle (mostly kind) watching from around the fire, I walk, wavering into the darkness. Beneath a big tree, near the ghats, in the lapping stillness of the water's edge, I lay my body down. *(My breathing had become agitated, and it took me a moment to become calm. The sound of the water was soothing and helped me re-center and continue.)*

(Death and Afterlife) As I gaze into the leafy canopy, a strange light dawns and my mother, long-since dead, beckons to me. There are others with her in the golden-red light stretching their arms out lovingly to me. With a gentle joyous shake, I rise up to meet them, and for only a moment, look back at the ragged form lying still and small beneath the tree. Gods and goddesses throng the sky now, Ganesh, Vishnu, Krishna, Sita, and my mother and father, lovers and friends. I am young and healthy again as I float up and up.

My family is under the protection of Shiva, the god with hair in a top knot with the crescent moon in it. He is huge, fifty feet tall, and we barely come up to his calves. We dart quickly through his legs, and see that others are not as fortunate as we and are being crushed beneath his feet as he dances destruction for the wicked. I feel guided by hands pulling me along and surrender to the flow. Beyond the giant dancing Shiva, the light is golden and clear; and soon we are moving out into midnight-blue space, or perhaps it is water. This is the lotus-land; for everywhere, like stars sprinkled in the sky, lotuses are gleaming. We are each given a lotus to sleep in, and we rock gently on the black lake, resting and rejuvenating in the fragrance of the flowers. How long we sleep here I do not know, but it feels pleasantly long enough, and when we begin to awaken, sit up and stretch, a giant hand plucks the lotuses and makes a bouquet of my family and friends.

We are carried in our blossoms into a great palace and placed in a bowl of water in a green room. We sit in the center of our lotuses and talk together, telling the stories of our lives, and what we liked and want more of, and what we disliked and how we would like to avoid the unpleasantness. As each one is speaking, the rest live into their story, uniting their souls and experiencing everything. Then we dream and envision how we want our next lives to be. As soon as we are satisfied with our creation, the goddess comes again. I am a tiny fairy elf-sized being in the heart of the lotus, which is lifted into the air as the goddess begins to dance. She takes a lotus in each hand, and dances the pattern of the life to be. Certain forms and patterns of energy are set in motion in my body, which I will remember kinesthetically in incarnations to come. The relationships between people are traced in the ethers and locked away in our bodies. She is beautiful and loving—Mahadevi, Queen of Heaven. When we have all been danced, she reverently pours the lotuses into the river of time and we float down over a waterfall and into a whirlpool. From this vortex, we will be born into life again. We wave farewell, feeling love and compassion, wishing one another well, and as we sink down, we begin to forget. Although we know we will meet again, and the feelings are good and happy, everything begins to blur and melt into unconsciousness. And so we slip, unaware, into incarnation again. *(The feeling and tone of the session began to change at this point. The following passages were not so much remembrance as a deeper understanding of the meaning of the experiences.)*

(Planning and Reincarnation) The people in my bouquet had integrity. We were gentle, kind, and devout, experiencing glimmers of the spiritual worlds in our prayers, offerings, and meditations. Having been decent human beings with a meaningful religious component in our former lives, we felt a certain security and trust in the benevolent workings of karma, and an excited anticipation for the adventures of the life to come. Dance was a driving motive in my last life and is planned for the one to come, as well. I wanted to be more in control of my next life, so I chose to be a male, but one who dances; a ceremonial warrior, Gangaji. My former mother, who had died when I was a young girl in the last life, is my wife whom I love in a highly respectful, deeply caring, delicate manner. Others from my bouquet are close to me again. Gangaji died in a holy war; this time after sleeping in the lotus, he was picked by a powerful god, and the bouquet was placed in a red room. *(After the stories of Nataranja and Gangaji came to their endings, I chose to stay in the spiritual worlds and review the after-death, ask questions of the deities, and come to a deeper understanding of human life and death and the spiritual background of ancient India.)*

(Conceptual Overview: a continuation of the spiritual hypnotherapy session) As the experiences of Nataranja and Gangaji faded, I was lifted to cosmic heights and could see that

the lotus-land and the colored rooms and palaces were different planes, different planets and worlds within our universe. The relationships were seen as patterns of energy flow. The river of time into which all lotuses are returned is on the moon, and the vortex of reincarnation is like a waterfall and whirlpool from the moon to the earth *(like the tunnel in an NDE).*

All this took place long, long ago; long before Christ, long before Buddha, in the mists and mystery of the beginning of human development in the cradles of culture on the Indian subcontinent. The Hindu gods were alive and powerful movers in human destiny, and were responsible for the evolution of human souls. They were tremendously huge, and lived in many different palaces and gardens in other realms. Each god and goddess had areas of activity that they influenced, and feelings that they inspired. They worked on the earth through the caste system. Each caste had a certain task, a specific initiation, a particular lesson to be learned in life, and human souls remained within the Hindu system until all castes had been experienced and all lessons learned.

Every soul that crossed the threshold of death had to pass between the dancing legs of Shiva, the Destroyer. Because this was in the beginning of time, most souls were new or very young without many previous incarnations, so the negative load of karma was comparatively small. Shiva danced on all negativity and crushed the evil from men's hearts. Most souls escaped destruction, like the group in which Nataranja found herself. They were only brushed and buffeted, to be cleansed of their mostly innocent sins of unkindness and thoughtlessness. People who had taken the "left-hand path" of black magic, or caused others suffering through volitional acts of violence, were destroyed beneath his pounding feet.

Each soul then experienced a time of rest and cosmic sleep in a lotus blossom, to heal and prepare for the new life. When the soul awoke, its lotus was picked by a god or goddess, the protector of the past life and caste, and brought into a colored room with others of their karmic circle. The rooms were porticoes, with only an inner wall or two, and open to a veranda. The roof was held up by large ornate pillars. The air was soft and warm, and the light diffuse.

Different gods gathered different kinds of bouquets, according to the nature and caste of the coming life. The pattern of the new life was danced into the souls and intensified by the colors of the clothing of the deity and the environment, and by music specific to the god or goddess. Music was designed to intensify each of the different stages of development. Warriors were bathed in a red glow with particularly strong rhythmic ragas, and their god was a powerful, noble, richly armored warrior, Indra. Humble middle-class workers and farmers were in green with a fertility goddess. Ascetic sadhus were in the presence of an ash-covered demon and cacophony. In the spirit world, between lives, the human soul at this time in history received imprints of color, sound, kinesthetic patterns, and religious impressions, which would impact the coming lifetime. These spiritual experiences were stimulated and remembered on earth each time the human being saw the color, experienced the movement or mudhra, sang or played particular music, prayed or meditated, or entered a temple to the guiding god or goddess.

In this way the lesson of the caste and the initiation into the earthly remembrance of the spiritual reality behind all things was embedded in the human psyche, and the caste system served the function of progressive evolutionary teachings in the outer world. It was the religious school system appropriate for the time, and the caste one was born into accurately reflected one's stage of soul development. It operated impartially through the law of karma, which at the beginning of the world was far less complicated than it is now in the twenty-first century.

It took many thousands of years and hundreds of reincarnations into successively higher castes for a soul to learn the fundamental earth lessons, and to experience a broad base of human emotions, thoughts, and actions. Gradually life became richer, relationships more complex, and people had more choice. The last incarnations in the Hindu series were as a Brahmin, under the tutelage of the golden father-god, Brahma. In ancient times, Brahmins were spiritually advanced souls, who remembered the divine in all earthly things; and who by their powerful presence reminded open-hearted people of their own divine potential. The initiation of the golden god was to open the Brahmin as a chalice or channel to direct guidance from the spiritual world through the practices of ablution, prayer, fasting, meditation, and service in the temples. After spending the appropriate number of Brahmin incarnations, the soul could choose to move into a different stream of evolution, such as those developing in the Middle East or Asia.

Conditions are different now in the spiritual world, just as they are very different on earth. The Hindu gods are smaller, and the globalization of potential incarnation has changed the relationship of gods to the souls in their care. The caste system no longer functions spiritually, but has become a socio-political force for the subjugation of the free individuality of our times. Human beings have evolved, and acquired faculties and abilities that were impossible even to conceptualize in ancient times. However, music, color, fragrance, movement, and mudhra still have the power to evoke reminiscences of times long gone and the spiritual worlds from which we came. They are, to this day, potent reminders of the spirit in all creation.

Culture had developed and life was becoming more complex when Nataranja lived and died. As the culmination of her spiritual training, she chose to recapitulate her life through dance. In her last hours, she remembered everything, felt and celebrated the joys and sorrows, and then released and let go into death. Remembering, reviewing, then releasing earthly issues while still alive on earth clears the path into the spiritual worlds. The principle of clearing life before death applies to the present time, as well. By working through issues and relationships, coming to forgiveness and acceptance; and in general, reflecting on each day and clearing the soul and mind of negative emotions before sleep, the work of the dissolution of the astral body in kamaloca is prepared and expedited while still alive.

CHAPTER 4

Confucianism

For centuries, the structure of Chinese life, including governmental organization, religious practices, and personal and familial behavior, was patterned after the writings of Confucius, who was born in 551 B.C. and died 479 B.C. He was a contemporary of Siddhartha Gautama Buddha and Lao Tzu. At fifty years of age he left his career as a government official, to begin thirteen years of travel and spiritual search.

His teachings were based on strict rituals for every facet of life. Nature was no longer the guide to organic human behavior. Now, formality and circumspection dictated relationships and structured the culture. The obligatory ties continued beyond death for as many as five familial generations.

The meticulous, exacting ideals of formally prescribed ceremony affected the afterlife. Before Confucius, the concept prevailed in China that the dead go to a dim subterranean realm, the Yellow Springs, a place of dry, dusty waiting. As Confucianism spread and all human activity became more limited by convention, so too did the experiences beyond death.

Spiritual Regression: *Chinese Male in Hunan Province and a Mercenary in the same area*

The following journey exemplifies Confucian beliefs and conventions in life and death. The traveler is the author, who has very little personal knowledge of Confucian beliefs or practices.

(The induction was a gentle relaxation and a set of stairs leading down, which brought me to a large compound, partially paved, with square, flat stones around the perimeter)

(Past Life) I am a little boy wearing Chinese pajama-clothes (silk pants and jacket). I have a little black hat on my head and a long braid down my back, a queue. I am running in the yard, chasing geese and ducks, but I am the son of the owner of the house and farm, the wealthy landowner.

Our religion is a kind of ancestor worship; it's very formal. I live in (speaks a name in a foreign tonal language which sounds like *Din* [spoken high] *Buan* [very inflected] China.) I see a map now; it's somewhat near the coast and a large city, but we have farms inland in gently rolling countryside. *(After the session I consulted a map of China; I believe that this incarnation took place in Hunan Province just inland from the coastal city of Fuzhou.)* It's temperate. In the winter, there might be a light dusting of snow, but not a lot. I live with my family. I have sisters but I am the only son. Later there will be a little brother.

I like the big room in our house that is the altar room. It is large with a high ceiling, and no one goes in there very often. I am only a child, but I put little grains of rice in various places on the altar, and sometimes flowers or feathers. I love the feathers from the geese and ducks in the courtyard, and I place these treasures in the best places on the altar. I bow silently, I don't sing or chant. It is nice because it is so quiet and still here. The air is dusty and thick and I don't make much noise at all. I don't want to disturb whatever is here. *(As I observed within the session, the air became thick and it felt as though discarnate people were beginning to precipitate or coalesce in the very atmosphere.)* I see people in the shadows; the ancestors are in this room in the shadows. That's why I like it here. The way the light comes in little slivers, I can see the old grandfather and my mother. She died and waits here. My father took a second wife, a concubine; and those are only my half-sisters, and she will have the second son.

As I grow older, I am busier, and my studies with my tutor in the library of our house take up my time. I don't go to the altar room much any more. I'm in my teens now and I don't come much at all; my mother who waits for me is very sad. The ancestors miss my visits. I have stayed in contact with them, but my mother looks a little reproachful and sad when I do come now, and that makes it difficult for me.

Since my father is quite wealthy, I am learning to take over the farms and the business, and the accounting. My family is looking for a bride for me now, and I like the idea. They want to find a girl who is very highly placed also—they want to make an advantageous marriage. But because I liked to run around all the time when I was younger, I don't want a girl with bound feet. I have a real repulsion to bound feet. However, there is not a single girl in my social class who does not have bound feet.

Now I am married, and we continue to live in my father's house. He gets old, and I take over the business; he stays, and my sisters who have not married stay too. My wife is lovely and skilled in the courtesan arts, and we have children. But we do not really have very much of a bond. We don't really connect. She is introverted and twisted because of what it is to be a woman; there is not much scope for her, so she is not very interesting. I am gone a lot; looking over the farms and property, and making sure things are sold at the big market that is far away in the city. We sell rice, melons, orchard produce, plums, and beans.

I have forgotten about the altar room now, until I am driven to the altar by unhappiness because everything is permeated by a dissociated feeling. I am happier in the city, and when I am there, I go to the pleasure houses, and there is one woman I have a passion for. However, I am taken advantage of. I'm drunk in the pleasure house of my favorite geisha, and wagers and contests are going on. I lose quite a lot of money, everything from this year's crops. *(Because I know only the common Japanese word for "courtesan," that was the term I used in the journey.)*

When I come back home in disgrace, my wife is screaming at me. I go into the altar room, and my mother is a little bit sharp with me. She says I have forgotten all the good things in life and I should have never stopped coming here. So I make vows to try to live a better life, but I have to sell many of the things in the house in order for everyone to survive though the winter. I am gripping my life anew. I am not drinking. I have learned that I want to be clear because of this whole disaster, and I am ashamed. Things do improve. Now we must all be very careful and frugal; but when I ask my wife what she needs to be happy, she decides to go back to visit with her own family for a while. I am actually very relieved. *(My wife was very disgusted with me, and I knew when she left that she would not return. The whole experience was actually painful during the session because of the rancor she poured out on me in that lifetime.)*

(Death and Afterlife) There has been some sort of an accident. I am bleeding and injured. I think it has been set up. As I was checking things in the barn, a whole wall of tools and blades fell on me, and I will die soon from the bleeding. As I lie in the growing pool of my own blood, I have the feeling that my life is hollow. There is no core or center to it. It was all outer and periphery, a personal and spiritual void. Life was all prescribed actions and behaviors, which is why I liked to be drunk. That's where the alcohol came in; to get beyond it all, to break free for a time.

As I am dying in the dust, straw and blood on the floor, my mother comes to me. She says that I did well in my life, but there is no one left who will revere me. I have no son, just a couple of young daughters. My father is still alive, in his dotage, and very, very old. My mother has been waiting for me in the altar room, but there will be no one for me to wait for: I loved no one and no one loved me. My mother and I go together hand in hand, along a misty, dusty hallway which reminds me of the feelings in the altar room until we come to a gate with a gatekeeper. Because I am young yet, and I have not lived a whole lifetime (I am only thirty-eight), I will go on. My mother wants to go back to the altar room and wait for my father, her husband.

I go through the gate and on to a place for people who have died young by accidents. My death was sort of an accident, although it is a question whether or not the nails were loosened so the things would fall. Whatever the reason, I did not die of old age. Everyone here looks like they did when they died. Whatever wounds they had are still apparent here, and we must learn how to fix them. I am covered with cuts and bruises all over me. I need to heal my spiritual (after-death) body. Because I died of loss of blood, I go to the Blood Goddess—a woman all in red. She sews up my cuts, and laughs, and says, "Having lost all your blood, you are easier to sew up; but of course, you couldn't have real blood in heaven anyway." So she puts red fire in my veins instead, a transparent red life-force. When she is finished, I walk out of that room and go through a kind of curtain at the doorway. The curtain is little strips of something like water coming down and I'm all healed when I come through.

Then I go to a room where I must make hand prints for identification. I go into another room and sit at a desk and do calligraphy· I write my version of the story of what happened in my life. It is like a life review. I write it all down. I say the things I did like and those I did not. I hesitate to accuse anyone of my death; but then I hear the mocking laughter of my wife, and I know that she had people arrange the accident. So then I say, "I'm glad anyway because life was not a happy thing for me." When I finish writing the life, I realize that I was happy as a child, but then things got so distant. I did not even bond with my own children. As girls, they were so much like their mother, and she and I did not do well together.

I have to separate the papers of what I did like and what I did not like, and give them to somebody who weighs them on a scale. The heavy ones, the dark, unpleasant pages go down and the light happy ones go up, proving that there wasn't much happiness in that life. I was not malicious; I just made mistakes, and did foolish things. I was stupid, but I was not mean-spirited. Because of the mistakes, I go to a time of being scourged and atoning for my stupidity and for the sorrow that my foolishness caused. Part of the foolishness was in being gullible and listening to that courtesan I lusted after, because she was not a good woman. She was out for money and for whatever she could get; and ultimately, that brought a lot of sorrow to everyone. When I see all that (and this is the first time I realized the depths of the truth about the geisha and my stupidity), it feels right that I should feel pain for what I did to cause my family suffering and humiliation. *(Humiliation is not a common experience for me in this present life, but I felt it to my very bones, when he realized his gullibility and the ridiculous choices he had made.)*

In the end, when the scourging is over, I go back to the red goddess, who sews up the new wounds. All the scourging and healing took place through a door on the left side of the weighing judge, where the dark pages were. Now I come back and go through a door on the right side where the white pages, the good pages, are. Here, I can live all the good things. I see my happiness as a child. I see my promise and potential as a young husband before my soul became twisted. And I really see the happiness in the altar room with my mother. I also loved walking in the fields, in nature and on the farms. The big city is not here at all.

I see that there was a girl, a servant or farm girl in our household that I really did love. She had big feet and she ran around, and we played as children. I see that the hollowness inside me existed because it was never filled with the love that would have been possible with her. I feel a great dissatisfaction with the system that dictates so much of one's life, and decrees that you can marry only within the same social standing. I feel cheated by not having had my own soul choose what I wanted to do and be.

At that point, a little orange-robed monk comes and taps on my papers as I am looking over them and reliving the experiences. I think he is here to remind me not to stray too far; it must be time to move on because I am not only reliving the happy times but I am going into deeper reflection. I get up and follow him back through the door to a large god-like Judge-Being with the white and black papers, and stand in front of him. He says, "Now you can choose again." And I reply, "I'm through choosing these things: what else can you offer?"

Then I go into a room where I can look down on the world and see the whole of life; what it is and where it is, and various possibilities. I am drawn to the same area of the world; I see China. I could choose to be a samurai or a geisha, or a businessman again; or I could choose to be almost anything, but a lot of things do not light up very well for me. Some scenarios are clear and some are dim and obscure. I felt so powerless in that last life because I felt so empty, that I am now deciding to be a warrior, and to have a certain amount of freedom and a strong sense of physical power and personal identity. I feel hopeful that with a stronger sense of self, I can find more happiness and satisfaction in this life to come.

41

I go over to a long table with a bulletin board on the wall where a spiritual being is working. I choose little pieces of paper from the bulletin board which indicate the characteristics, features and abilities for my next life. The being takes all the little papers and bundles them up and drops them down a chute/tube to earth. I watch for a moment as my creation, the fetus, begins to develop and then it is time for me to go into a darkened room and lie down and go to sleep.

(Reincarnation) I wake up as a robust baby boy of about two years of age. I am very strong and stocky, and I live on one of the farms from the last life, although it has been 100 years, earth-time, since that last incarnation. *(This fact was "told" to me during the session. I heard, "It's been 100 years.")* I was "found" by a samurai/warrior trainer when I was in my early teens, because my reputation for strength and bravado was spreading through the countryside. I was schooled in the art of fighting. I lived a lusty life, sweeping the peasant girls off their big feet as a free-lance protector and lover, and then was recruited for a border war. I died in a skirmish, when a curved sword went through the plates of my leather armor, and straight into my heart. I had a bit more freedom in this life and felt a swaggering sense of self, but there was no depth.

This Confucian journey shows the general pattern of the afterlife very clearly: life review; recognition and resolution of mistakes and misdeeds, as well as celebration of joys; realization and integration; and then choosing new impulses for the next incarnation. This afterlife journey clearly demonstrated the workings of karma, transformation, and reincarnation. In this case, these workings were all clothed in the culture of ancient China and embedded within the Confucian world paradigm.

The process of understanding what is visibly, aurally, or intuitively perceived during a hypnotherapy session varies.

Some experiences are easily described and some are more subtle and difficult to express. Spiritual worlds are timeless and spaceless, so it is only through metaphor and example that one can perceive and understand what is happening. In the narrations of past lives, modern objects and concepts sometimes present themselves, and language discrepancies are common. Examples of this here are pajamas and bulletin boards in ancient Confucian China. *Geisha* and *samurai* are not Chinese, but Japanese words now in common usage. Travelers describe people, places, and experiences in terms of their own personal perceptions, and within the present cultural context. Certainly the traveler's psychology is a genuine factor in the retrieval of the afterlife experience. However, the emotional and dramatic content of the experiences reflects causal reality that can be followed into subsequent incarnations, as shown in the story above.

CHAPTER 5

Buddhism

Buddhism is based on the enlightened revelations of Siddhartha Gautama, born in 563 B.C. in what is now Nepal. His father was the ruler of a small kingdom. Prince Siddhartha lived a protected life of luxury, married Princess Yasodhara, and had one son. His discontent and first awakening are told in the story of *The Four Passing Sights*, in which Siddhartha confronted old age, disease, death, and the Hindu path of renunciation.

Horrified by the brutality of the human condition, Siddhartha left his wife, son, palace, and kingdom to seek enlightenment. For six years, in three phases, he devoted himself totally to awakening. He did that first by following Hindu Masters to learn the teachings and read the sacred scriptures; second, by becoming an extreme ascetic. At the end of that path, he realized the futility of such extremes. And last, he practiced *Raja Yoga*, the path of psycho-physical exercise: physical postures, yoga, meditation, concentration of body and mind.

As the result of his life experiences, Siddhartha developed the "Middle Way" between the extremes of indulgence and asceticism. On the full moon in May, he sat beneath a Bodhi tree, determined to achieve enlightenment. He was assailed by temptation from Mara, the Evil One (death incarnate), but overcame all, remaining in perfect concentrated meditation.

He achieved the "Great Awakening," disappearing as Siddhartha into union with God and becoming the Buddha. He taught for nearly half a century. Buddha died at eighty years of age in 483 BC.

The Four Noble Truths and the Eightfold Path

The Four Noble Truths and the Eightfold Path are the distilled wisdom of his enlightenment. They are the foundation of all Buddhist teachings.

1. Life is suffering.
2. The cause of suffering is the habituated desire for individual satisfaction, at the expense of others if necessary.
3. The cure for this suffering is liberation from selfishness, and a wider world view.
4. The way from suffering to liberation is the Eightfold Path.

The Eightfold Path is an expression of the Golden Rule: do unto others as you would have them do unto you. It is a practical approach to moral living leading to enlightenment. The preliminary step to the path is right association, keeping the company of like-minded friends. In this prerequisite, the path has a social and communal imperative, as well as being a vehicle for individual enlightenment.

1. *Right Knowledge* is a circle with the Four Noble Truths because the fourth noble truth is the Eightfold Path, and the first step on that path is knowledge of the Four Noble Truths.
2. *Right Aspiration* means to decide on liberation as the goal and then to pursue it throughout life.

3. *Right Speech* focuses on the language of truth.
4. *Right Behavior* is based on the ethical Five Precepts:
   Do not kill.
   Do not steal.
   Do not lie.
   Do not be unchaste.
   Do not take drugs or drink intoxicants.
5. *Right Livelihood* encourages ethical occupations which promote life rather than destroy it.
6. *Right Effort* is moral exertion.
7. *Right Mindfulness* is continuous self-examination, which keeps the mind in control of the senses and impulses, rather than being driven by them.
8. *Right Absorption* involves the techniques of *raja yoga*. The result is regeneration and a new world view.

There are many sects of Buddhism; and correspondingly, many different beliefs about the after-death experience. I have chosen to concentrate on Tibetan or Vajrayana Buddhism because it has spread around the world and is a potent influence in the West.

A key to understanding the Vajrayana Buddhist philosophy and worldview is the concept of the complete circle of existence, from birth through life and death to a new rebirth. The environments and events of life are obvious, but the other half of the circle, death, is not so clear. However, *The Bardo Thodrol* (also known as *The Tibetan Book of the Dead* or *The Great Liberation through Hearing in the Bardo*) is a guide book to those unknown regions. It presents descriptions of landscapes and beings in the realms of death and directs the deceased soul to the proper paths.

The Bardos

The Tibetan word *bardo* means a transition between relatively stable states of existence. These transitions or gaps in the seamless flow of illusion and delusion are moments of chaos and change, when the discerning mind can break through the facade of appearance to the eternal verity of the clear light of the pure mind. Existence is a circle made of four quarters, the four bardos: (1) The Natural Bardo of Life, (2) The Painful Bardo of Dying, (3) The Luminous Bardo of Dharmata, and (4) The Karmic Bardo of Becoming.

The bardos or transitional states can be described as follows:

(1) *The Natural Bardo of Life* may seem more than just a bardo or a transition to each of us who are alive at this moment. But from a larger point of view, it is only a small but very important time in which to prepare for death and all the other bardos.

Existence does not stop at death but reveals itself thereafter as the clear unencumbered state of "pure mind" where one can reside as in Nirvana, or from whence incarnations precipitate anew. It is through the mind at rest, in its essential simplicity, that death is accepted and overcome. Our own mind is the door to enlightenment.

"Mind" is not an isolated human phenomenon, although it is with our personal mind and thinking that we at first apprehend the larger concepts of life and death. They are both in the mind, intimately bonded; and each affects the other. His Holiness the Dalai Lama says, "If we wish to die well, we must learn how to live well; hoping for a peaceful death, we must cultivate peace in our mind, and in our way of life." With practice, and ultimately through attainment of enlightenment or death, whichever comes first, primal reality is experienced.

The goals of the Tibetan Buddhist way are liberation and enlightenment. Liberation means freedom from the bondage of illusion, and from the neurotic veils of addiction, habit and fear. Enlightenment is the state of having received spiritual insight that leads to the recognition of true reality. Also known as illumination, enlightenment lights up all aspects of existence and achieves union with the clear light and truth.

The means by which humanity achieves the goals of liberation and enlightenment are "reincarnation" and "karma." Reincarnation is the necessary continuation of life after death, after life after death, to learn all the lessons of existence and perfect all the disciplines which lead to eventual liberation and enlightenment. The magnitude of life and evolutionary developments cannot be experienced in one lifetime alone. As Voltaire quipped, "It is no more surprising to be born twice than it is to be born once." Multiple lives over eons of time are necessary for an individualized Ego/I consciousness to perceive, master, and transcend the human condition, and to achieve liberation and enlightenment.

Karma is the tool for manifesting the lessons in each life. It is the means by which the adage, "as you sow, so shall you reap" is actualized. The result of an action or thought is held within its execution. Every event is pregnant with its own conclusion and is perfectly balanced; every cause has an effect and every action a consequence. Karma is the law of compensation. This impartial, impersonal concept must then be applied to the reality of everyday life, if we wish to understand the effect the law of karma has on each individual. What comes to us is engendered by our own past actions. Our freedom of response to the manifest reality that karma brings, results in positive or negative experiences in this life and karma for the future.

In this natural bardo of life, meditative practice creates the possibility of choice. Meditation clears emotions; breaks the attachments we have to self-limiting habits of control; and offers a relatively clear space in which to experience our own truth. Meditation inserts a break between cause and instinctive reaction, and affords the opportunity for considered, conscious response. Meditation, yoga, and other disciplines and religious practices are tools for moderating karma and affecting both life and death.

The P'howa empowerment, in particular, is an experiential meditation guiding the practitioner though the transference of consciousness at the moment of death into the "Pure Land of Amitabha Buddha." It is a discipline to still the mind and direct rebirth as a continuation toward enlightenment. During life, the process includes daily exercises that purify the mind for a stronger, more effective P'howa practice at death.

(2) *The Painful Bardo of Dying* takes place in stages. It begins with the first throes of death, and ends when all outer physical processes have ceased, and when all inner states of emotion and thought have dissolved as well.

In the beginning, the outer senses cease to function; the ears no longer hear; the eyes no longer see; none of the senses register any stimulus. The next phase of outer dissolution is a letting go of relationships to the elements. The process of dying is the rarefying of the heavier elemental qualities into the next higher frequency, until the mind is finally free of all lower vibrations and manifests as the "Ground Luminosity," the clear white light. The elements of earth, water, fire, and air are progressively released. When finally the air element withdraws and the breathing ceases altogether, the outer dissolution is complete.

The "inner dissolution," which is said to elapse in approximately twenty minutes, is completed when all thoughts and emotional states are resolved through four increasing subtle levels.

After the outer and inner dissolutions, the mind is separated from the body at death. The true nature of the mind is then revealed as the Ground Luminosity or the Buddha Nature, which is described as the boundless light of pure consciousness, and the eternal realm of infinite truth. This is the first and prime opportunity to achieve liberation and avoid the necessity for further reincarnation. However, most humans are overcome by the immensity and awesome power of the Ground Luminosity; or they have no prior life experience of meditation or transcendent states, and so are bewildered or frightened. Meditative concentration in the reality of the Ground Luminosity is then broken and the soul separates out again. The opportunity to remain at one in the heart of the Buddha in an eternal state of enlightenment has passed, and the soul now begins the downward spiral toward reincarnation.

The Tibetan Book of the Dead is designed to assist the human mind in remaining peacefully conscious through the experiences beyond death, in not indulging in attraction or avoidance, but remaining neutral and aware. Passages are read to the dying to remind them of the nature of the mental states they are experiencing, the signs and symbols they may perceive, and to assist them in making appropriate choices. The state of equanimity thus achieved keeps the soul from being drawn into the dramas of negativity and passion that seem so real and enticing. If liberation from the illusions of karmic necessity is not experienced at this point, then the human soul is drawn into ever deepening stages of death, and at last is compelled into rebirth. However, the possibility of perceiving the clear light of mind behind all of the succeeding visions and images arises at each successive stage, affording many opportunities for liberation or a fortunate birth.

(3) _The Luminous Bardo of Dharmata_ encompasses the after-death experience of the radiance of the nature of mind, the luminosity or Clear Light, which manifests as sound, color, and light. This is the heart of death. The Bardo of Dharmata comprises four stages: (a) Luminosity, (b) Union with the Deities, (c) Wisdom, and (d) Spontaneous Presence.

(3.a) In Luminosity or The Landscape of Light, the whole field of perception is brilliant with light, color, and sound. If one can meditate in this state and create stability, it will remain as long as the meditation lasts.

(3.b) During the time of Union with the Deities, the light and color of the Luminous Landscape of Light begins to coalesce and form patterns. The mandalas depict the five "wisdoms"—the five modes of energy of the buddhas or awakened ones. In the center of the mandala is the embodied god of the particular virtue with his consort, and surrounding or below are the associated gods and goddesses. This phase of Dharmata takes approximately seven days, although the "day" is measured in meditative time, not a twenty-four hour period. The time spent with each deity depends upon the individual's capacity to remain clear, at peace, and focused. Many _tankas_ (Buddhist paintings) depict these deities, and meditating on them in life is preparation for a successful passage through this aspect of the bardo.

Reading _The Bardo Thodrol_ to the departed at this time is also very important. The material reminds the discarnate soul of the various stages and the appropriate responses in each phase. The name of the deceased is called and the soul is spoken to directly; the passage is explained in detail. The mandala visions are described and the simultaneous allure of the negative aspect is warned against. It is important to know and remember that all the deities, whether beneficent or ferocious, are all projections of the mind.

Each "day" is spent in the abode or energy field of successive families or clans of deities.

The First Day: Vairocana—The Buddha Family, Center, White.

The Second Day: Vajrasattva or Aksobhya—The Vajra Family, Water, Blue.

The Third Day: Ratnasambhava—The Ratna (Jewel) Family, Earth, Yellow.

The Fourth Day: Amitabha—The Padma (Lotus) Family, Fire, Red.

The Fifth Day: Amoghasiddhi—The Karma Family, Air, Green.

The Sixth Day: The Peaceful Deities—At the conclusion of the individual elements, the forty-two peaceful divinities appear simultaneously in a vast mandala.

The Seventh Day: The Wrathful Deities—At this time the virtues or positive qualities of the five wisdoms are transformed into their opposites, ferocious wrathful deities *(herukas)* with three heads and six arms, dramatically portraying the extreme energy of the negative sides. Throughout this horrifying encounter, the dead must remember that the wrathful deities are in truth, only projections of their own minds, as were the wise and beautiful ones.

(3.c) In the Bardo of Dharmata, Wisdom transcends all possible negativity. The five forms of wisdom (Wisdom of the All-Encompassing Space, Mirror-Like Wisdom, Equalizing Wisdom, Wisdom of Discernment, and All-Accomplishing Wisdom) are displayed in divine light.

(3.d) Spontaneous Presence is the symbolic vision of total reality in all planes of existence. After the Spontaneous Presence has filled all space, it fades and dissolves back into its original essence.

Throughout all of the experiences of the Luminous Bardo of Dharmata, a person's own subjective relationship to the benign and wrathful deities and to the colors and displays of the mind influences what is perceived. Our self-delusions obscure our perception of reality in these otherworldly dimensions, as they did in life. Our own habits and karmic predispositions cloud our perception of the true luminosity. If we cannot overcome our tendencies from the past lifetime, they will create their own future.

(4) *The Karmic Bardo of Becoming* lasts from the time the soul leaves Dharmata until the moment of the new birth, which can be from one week to forty-nine days. The soul moves from the purer states of the radiance of the Ground Luminosity and Dharmata to the denser forms of mental energy as the first step in the process of re-becoming. What takes place at this stage is a reversal of the former process of dissolution. Thought states which include negativity now begin to accrete to the karmic residue of the past life and cohere into mental faculties for the new incarnation; consciousness begins to dawn.

Two further experiences in the Bardo of Becoming are first, a reliving of the past life; and second, a judgment. There is an unrolling of all the experiences of the life just past; all memories, all perceptions and all sensations. In this life review of the past, old patterns that still cling are the basis for the next life's issues.

The judgment scene is a common theme in many religions and cultures. In the Tibetan Buddhist tradition, the good and bad actions from life are tallied by little white and black stones, held by a white angel and a black imp. The judgment is actually meted out by ourselves and is simply the just results of our own actions. We are the judge of our own mindset, either forgiving and understanding, or harsh and judgmental.

If rebirth is inevitable, because liberation has not been experienced in any of the higher bardo states, there are rituals and teaching on how to close the womb; or finally, on choosing a fortunate incarnation. Karmic necessity in the form of attraction and instinct pull the soul into one life realm or another. At this point, descent into a body can be very rapid and unconscious. The circle is complete and one has entered again the Natural Bardo of Life.

Spiritual Regressions: Selection of After-Death Sessions with Buddhists in India.

I facilitated spiritual hypnotic sessions for a number of Tibetan Buddhists while I was in India, including three monks. All three lamas and many of the others experienced former lives and deaths as Buddhists. A translator was necessary for a few, so the descriptions are sometimes in the third person. Although none of the sessions contained the whole journey as described in the *Bardo Thodrol,* many of the elements were experienced in symbolic form. The bardo in which the experience takes place is indicated by italics in parentheses.

I am dying. I am a monk wearing yellow robes and Tibetan boots. I am in meditation, seeing God all around. There is a spinning chakra on my head. Outside the room, all the lamas are doing *puja* (prayers). I feel myself dying; as I die I hear the lamas telling me that I am dying. It is night and the full moon is shining. The lamas are reading The Bardo Thodrol. *(Ritual of Reading to the Dead)* I see the funeral and feel my body in a box.

Now I am seeing fire. *(Lotus Family)*

Now I am flying in the wind. *(Karma Family)*

Now there is rainfall. *(Vajra Family)*

Now the monastery is being destroyed as red water fills the *gompa* (the sanctuary) and it is sinking and being washed away. It has disappeared. All is gone. It is all in my mind, the destruction of the monastery, the fires, and the wheels spinning. It is a clear vision of the bardos in the mind.

❖

As I am dying, my daughter and son are crying and I say, "don't cry." A lama comes and makes *puja* (rituals and prayers), but too many people are crying and making noise and disturbing me so the lama makes them go away. In the stillness, then, my heart stops; no breathing, chest tight, but no pain. Consciousness leaves at the top of the head and goes to Amitabha Buddha *(P'howa Practice)*. There is melting, spinning and whirling in emptiness. There are no beings, only a lotus, colors and light.

❖

When I die, I rise up and see a smiling skeleton with worms crawling in it and I don't care. I am floating higher and higher and at first I have no form. Then I am sitting cross-legged in meditation posture. My body is light and I am dressed in silk. Suddenly, I disappear, exploded in thousands of pieces of light. I am light inside.

❖

She is in a Buddhist temple of the Japanese style, with a fish pond and a white statue and purple and blue lotus. She is inside the temple and she is herself only. Oh, but now she is wearing a yellow robe and shoes with toes that turn up. She was a teacher monk with a long beard and a great staff who has died. Now she is flying over the sea and seeing the lotus and *nagas* (snakes) and angels. She is flying with the angels, and silver is all over and white and blue, and sees golden houses. Now she is a peacock and sees the same lotus and Japanese temple. There are no red flowers, only purple, blue, and white. But now as she is flying again, she sees Eskimos on a sleigh down below and she wonders why.

Spiritual Regressions:

In the following two Tibetan journeys, the particular bardo in which the experience takes place is indicated by italics in parentheses.

Lifetime #1: *Tibetan Buddhist Monk and a Male in India in 1200 A.D.*

The timeless, unchanging quality of Tibetan life for so many centuries makes dating the following story difficult, although the succeeding incarnation took place in 1200. The traveler has had very little involvement with Tibetan Buddhism in this present life. She is, however, involved in meditative practices and is a hypnotherapist and psychologist.

(The induction was a classic body relaxation protocol and a flight of stairs going down. At the bottom of the stairs there was a little boat on a large and placid river.)

(Natural Bardo of Life) I ask to be ferried back to Tibet, and a boat with a big prow like a bird or dragon is there and the ferryman pushes off with a pole. I see people working in the fields on the banks. Then there are changes in the smell, the river is wilder, and mountains are rising high on both sides. The river is getting narrower and we are in a gorge. It is very quiet and we are still going upstream. Now we are pulling over to a muddy bank and I have to step into the mud with my bare feet. I am a young monk; I have a staff and I walk in the dank and misty landscape. My shaved head is cool because I am in a mountainous region and very high. I take the path into the mountains, and I am alone. I don't seem to have a particular intention; I am just walking and quite happy. Now I am coming out in a sunny area and it feels warmer. I sit and take out a piece of bread, my thoughts are only that "it is good; nothing is lacking."

As I sit in the sunlight, memories flood my mind. I was brought to the lamasery as a young boy. An older man, my grandfather, brought me there. My parents had died, and so my grandfather is bringing me and he is very proud to dedicate me in this way. I am a bit confused because I am so young. I have no conscious memory of my mother or father. I think there was a younger brother, too young for the lamasery yet. So I have grown up my whole life in the monastery.

One day there is a funeral; the most important monk is laid out, and the others are chanting around the body. I am between eleven and fourteen years old, and it is a big event to be allowed to watch and participate. He was someone I revered. There is a golden light that surrounds the body, but I also feel sadness. The teachings of our sect seem true to me. It all feels very familiar. I am also aware of a part of me that is carrying sadness because of the passing of those who have loved me. Impermanence is very clear, but there is also joy. I experience the practices as being very deep; but sometimes I feel young, and I want to just go out walking or to play.

After eating my bread, I continue on the path until I meet an old man. We stop; he knows me. He is pointing up the side of the mountain to a place I am to find and go sit in. It's strange to be without the other monks, but I have been sent out to do this thing alone. I don't know who this man is, but he looks familiar and I trust him. I go where he points, and I climb up the mountainside to a small cave in the rocks, with a ledge in front. I sit on the ledge and it is breathtaking, looking out at the mountains. I understand that I am to be here for some time. There is some trepidation and some peace.

I have been here for a long time and I have learned to love it. But now it is time to leave the cave and the ledge. It is hard to leave; it's like a pulling and a tearing because I have been here a few years. The treasure I am bringing back is Truth. I have achieved peace and truth. So I leave my beloved mountains and return to the lamasery and perform my duties for many more years.

(Death: the Bardo of Dying) I am in a small room; my body is old but not terribly old, and I had an illness. The other monks are tending to the needs of the body—smoke, fragrance, chanting, and recitation of texts. I know that what is happening is well-known. *(Ritual of Reading the Bardo Thodrol)*

I am beginning to feel the life force rising up, receding from the feet and coming to the upper parts of the body. I can observe what is happening and I am curious. I feel it moving up through the torso like a tide receding. It moves up toward my head and then out; I stay for a bit to observe the monks and the body, and I convey to them somehow that it is good and all is well, just as we have always taught. *(P'Howa Practice of the Transfer of Consciousness at the Moment of Death.)*

There is pulling or drawing up, a moving through some space where there is music, and I am floating in music. I see images of my beloved mountains, images of nature just passing by, all just floating by peacefully. *(Outer Dissolution)*

Next I go to a place where there is a long reflecting pool and trees around the courtyard that are shedding blossoms. It is my work to sweep them up and pick them out of the pool, and to do only this for a time. The assignment is to be invisible. The image is shedding attachments; shedding images, pictures, everything. I am sitting and doing practices of emptying. *(Inner Dissolution)*

I am coming up toward a great image of the Buddha, a seated Buddha with hand outstretched. It's a living Buddha, not a statue, and I am passing into the Buddha's heart, though I am not quite able to know there is no difference. Such radiance and splendor in coming to dwell in the heart of the Buddha for a time, just to rest. *(Luminous Bardo of Dharmata)*

And then I am reflecting, and assessing the life just lived, and I hear the words, "Well done." There is more; there is more to burn off. No need to pass through Hells anymore, no need to struggle, but more to burn off until there is no distinction between self and the heart of the Buddha. *(Life Review)*

The key to the Heart of the Buddha is a wordless space. Why is it always necessary to leave? Why leave the cave and the heart of the Buddha? Wherever this form is located, there is this burning and I must leave. *(She was very sad as she said this, as she felt this was a pattern in this present life as well.)*

Some people come who speak and teach, as in earth life, but purer now—not so many trappings; more essence. I have an awareness of the council of teachers. But it is a trick; they appear as an old man with goatee and gown, and a woman with long hair, but they are . . . *(She paused for a long while, then continued.)* I can see the flame in each one. The form is just an outer covering. It takes a flame to see a flame. Absolutely none of this is significant really, but the need to continue to come into reincarnation again to play it out. Members of this council seem to agree that there is a need to descend further into density in the next life so that more of the *clarifying* (like ghee from butter) might happen. *(Judgment)*

I am aware of my reluctance as I hear them, and a concern about forgetting. So they point to the flame inside me, and assure me that the outcome is not in question. And certain ones will appear along the way to provide links to remembrance.

So I see the shape of the life to come. It is the life in India. I see the descent into power and cruelty, abuse of power over others, and the choice at the end when the true teacher appears. One sees only the outline, and then one must make the choice to go. I have been in the spiritual worlds for several hundred years. Many years pass when one is in the heart of the Buddha.

There are others gathered to assist in the descent and embodying who say to me, "This is all the heart of the Buddha." As I am descending into reincarnation, there is still vastness. It's like going into a funnel, moving through layers slowly at first and then speeding up. As I pass the layers, I realize that the beloved mountains and nature are not to be in this next life. It will be in a civilized city in 1200 A.D. in India. *(Reincarnation: Return to the Natural Bardo of Life) (The client knew many of her past lives previous to our work together; hence she could see the next incarnation and know the timing.)*

Lifetime #2: *Shrimluck a Nomadic Buddhist Woman and a Child in America*

Again, the timeless quality of Tibetan life makes it challenging to date the sessions. This one is set somewhere not too long before the 1800's, because the traveler was able to observe covered wagons going west in America before the next incarnation. This traveler had no knowledge of Tibetan Buddhist practices in this life. She was a young science student in college.

(The induction brought the traveler down a narrow rocky path to a river, where a small boat was waiting. An old man motioned

her into the boat and set off upstream. He pulled ashore at
another rocky landing.)

(Natural Bardo of Life) I stepped out of the boat and was walking up a rocky path up a hill, surrounded by grassy plains. I'm wearing lots of woolen clothes and boots with pointy, turned-up toes. I am a middle-aged woman. I am coming home to a yurt tent-house and all the people come out to say "hello," and welcome me home. They are my extended family, including aunts and uncles; the entire clan lives here. We raise goats, and I am one of the many herders. Our yurt is big and round, and I sleep and eat here. Pretty much everything goes on in this place. There is a big pot for cooking over a fire and a woman is braiding another's hair. I feel pretty happy and included here, and I'm happy to be home.

There are no obvious religious signs or symbols here; there is a little altar with a Buddha, but it is not really important. The family group, the clan, is more important and supportive. The only religious impulses in this life are some daily rituals. I am bending over and dropping things and lighting candles and saying things, and when I do these rituals, I feel concentrated and focused.

(After exploring this scene, I suggested she move forward to the next important event in this life – which she did.)

I am sitting down with a man; we are on our knees, my hand is on something sacred, and his is on top of mine. He has dark skin and slanted eyes like everyone else. I feel separate and a little nervous, like I'm watching the whole marriage from afar. The clan is happy about it.

Now, I am having a baby, a boy. He is healthy and it was a fine birth. His name is Rajpud. *(At this point, the traveler and I both burst out laughing. "Rajpud," she said, "how can I name my darling baby Rajpud?" And we laughed hysterically till tears ran from our eyes. When we finally settled down, I just said, "And now easily and naturally, we can continue the story of you and*

62

little Rajpud." and she went on.) I am Shrimluk. I take my baby Rajpud out with me to tend the goats, first as a baby and then as a little boy with other little children in the clan. Sometimes, it's just me herding the goats and I like it. I feel free, I feel at ease and pretty comfortable. We are in Tibet or Outer Mongolia, nomadic, clan living, and matrilineal. Women have a strong role and I have a big responsibility; it is an honor to herd the goats. Our clan was very isolated.

(Death: The Bardo of Dying) I get sick. I live to be really old, and I die of natural causes. My husband had died long before me. He was not as old. He had an accident. I was not at his death, nor is he at mine. Rajpud is beside me and he is a grown man. The clan is there pouring water on my forehead and singing.

When my soul separates, it remains for a while at the pinnacle of the tent. My family is saying verses and singing songs to help to release my spirit, and it really helps. *(Ritual of Reading the Bardo Thodrol)* My death feels beautiful. They hold my hands, and the songs are very beautiful and help me unfurl and spiral upward. *(The traveler was awed and spoke in hushed tones, and a tear or two slipped from her eyes.)* I go up and through the tent, and I zoom up and up. Earth is getting smaller and smaller, and it's dark all over.

(Luminous Bardo of Dharmata) I have the image of a dry leaf being blown about in the wind. *(Amoghasiddhi: Karma Family—Air)* Then I'm walking up some stairs and it's light everywhere, very bright in contrast. I walk up stairs and I turn into liquid and am poured out on the ground; my shape disintegrates on the ground. *(Vajrasattva: Vajra Family—Water)* It's like an amoeba, and then it swirls up and becomes another human being and goes and walks down the steps. It was wind and breath and air that were effective to change the amorphous amoeba into a new form, a new person. *(Amoghasiddhi: Karma Family—Air)*

At the bottom of the rise, there are pit stairs that go down into the ground and lead back to darkness. I see the earth, but I wait and watch for a while. Looking down, I see the North American continent. Wagon trains are threading their way across the vast plains, and then are lost in the forests and mountains of the west. I watch while towns arise and grow to cities; now the earth is coming closer and closer.

(Bardo of Becoming) As I get close to the earth, I feel the element of water. I feel waves. Then I am squished through a small opening, arms first like diving, and there are bright lights like in a hospital, and it is much more present time, the 1920s maybe. It was a fast and short time in the spiritual world. I am now a little boy with a dog, wearing shorts and suspenders, and I have a toy boat on the river. The milk is delivered in bottles; and I'm in America. *(Reincarnation: Return to the Natural Bardo of Life.)*

It is clear from the Buddhist sessions that although the *Bardo Thodrol* describes a complete after-death journey, it is only a general outline. Each individual's beliefs, vocabulary, and evolutionary stage affect and color one's experiences on the other side. So far, this seems to hold true for all religions.

CHAPTER 6

Judaism and Islam

Judaism

Judaism, one of the worlds oldest traditions, begun by Abraham many millenia ago, has been an ever-changing religion encompassing a wide variety of beliefs and religious expressions. A belief in the intrinsic value of all experiences because they come ultimately from the Creator-God has been indispensable in face of the Diaspora and persecutions.

The after-death beliefs of Judaism evolved and transformed throughout the ages, as new faculties of soul and perception were developed in humanity. At times, certain sects of Judaism accepted reincarnation or resurrection, while others did not, giving rise to prolonged theological debates which were still occurring at the time of Christ's incarnation. However, the defining belief is that there is no afterlife. An example is the ancient description of the land of the dead as a "valley of dry bones," called *Sheol*, from which souls could never escape.

Though I facilitated many journeys for people of the Jewish faith, not one Jewish past life and after-death arose, other than my own past life and death in the Holocaust.

Islam

Muhammad was born into the leading tribe of Mecca in 570 AD and died in 632 AD. Arabia had been populated by the descendants of Ishmael, one of the sons of Abraham, the Father of the tribes of Israel. Although their roots were in the Old Testament of the Bible, in common with the Jews, a prophetic stream particular to Arabia had developed over the millennia. In Muhammad, this divergent philosophy culminated in the Koran, which is not only a religious text, but also a political guide and legal system. Islam is a severely monotheistic religion. The dogma of the orthodox Muslim religion does not accept the concept of reincarnation, and no former Islamic lives came to light among the many hypnotherapy journeys.

However, the Sufis, a mystical sect initiated by the poet Jalaladin Rumi, which includes the Mevlevi Whirling Dervishes, emphasizes the dying of the Self into the ecstatic consciousness of God in the midst of every action, every thought, and every moment; daily life is thus hallowed. Although I did not find a Sufi past life, this heretical poem by Rumi, gracefully sums up the Sufi belief in evolution through reincarnation.

> I died as mineral and became a plant,
> I died as plant and rose to animal,
> I died as animal and I was Man.
> Why should I fear? When was I less by dying?
> Yet once more I shall die as Man, to soar
> With Angels blest; but even from angelhood
> I must pass on . . .

CHAPTER 7

Exoteric Christianity

Christianity is based on the life, death, and resurrection of Jesus Christ. This pivotal figure of Christianity is considered to be both fully human and fully divine. The early Christian disciples experienced the compassion, equality, and transcendence of Jesus Christ's teachings and carried them out into the world. Christianity, now the largest religion in the world, is found in all parts of the globe. The resurrection of Christ after the crucifixion on Golgotha, is the prime basis of Christian theology.

The world can be seen as a dichotomy of the overt, the outer, and the hidden, the inner; that which is exterior and manifest to the senses, and that which is internal and alive in the soul. Since time immemorial, this fundamental division of reality has influenced spiritual and religious practices. The term *Exoteric* applies to outer religious practices and the authoritative dogma of the churches, and the term *Esoteric* applies to the "not for the public" information of spiritual significance of the imperceptable life of the soul; hence the division of Christianity into two distinct chapters in this book.

Most denominations of modern Christianity believe in a static afterlife of either Heaven or Hell. The deeds of this one lifetime (most exoteric Christians do not believe in reincarnation) consign the soul to either place, usually for eternity. Any other belief was (and is still) considered heretical by the Roman Catholic Church, which dominated Christianity for centuries.

Spiritual Regression: *Brother Matteus in Germany, 1400, and a French Huguenot, 1500*

The next journey takes place in the 1400s before the spread of the printing press. At that time there were a variety of Catholic sects with differing beliefs. This may account for the fact that this afterlife journey did not follow the strict dogma of the Roman Catholic Church. The life takes place in a monastery located in Southern Germany. The author is the traveler.

(The induction, after a relaxation protocol, took me up a flight of stairs, which is an unusual direction to travel at the beginning of a hypnotherapy session. However, it worked very well in this instance.)

(Past Life) I came up the dark stone stairway from the cellar and looked down at my fat old feet with the round little toes in sandals, and at my monk's habit and cowl. I was wearing a dirty white apron, and when I reached the light, I was aware that I had four bottles of wine in my arms. I walked slowly to the refectory of our monastery. The long wooden tables were still empty, so I put the bottles at the head of each and went out into the garden.

The sun felt good after the dark cellar; I closed my eyes as I sat on the bench in the herb garden, and leaned back against the ancient oak that threw a dappled shade. My brown habit absorbed the flickering sunlight and I warmed up quickly. I could hear the choir practicing in the chapel, and the clatter of pots and bowls in the kitchen. I was old and frail, though plump around the middle and I drifted off into reverie.

I had been here in this place almost all of my life. When I was a young novice, I had come to sing, and had stayed, directing the choir and cantoring on the holy days. At that time, I was afire with the love of Christ and the possibilities inherent in the human soul. The music moved me to ecstasy to the depths of my soul, and I felt intimations of the divine within myself. Intense new thoughts about God's grace toward humanity were sweeping some of the churches and monasteries, and a few monks and nuns had had transcendent visions and angelic visitations. Then I had felt divine joy in my singing and had been transported by the glory of the sunlight through the stained-glass windows. I was happy.

However, the abbot suspected heresy in the new revelation. A gaunt, hawk-nosed, sunken-eyed man, he continued to flagellate himself every night, believing that pain and suffering were the only way to Christ. We had been friends in school together, but our destinies took very different turns. At first, we talked about our experiences and beliefs. "Man is like the worms in the dust," he said. "But Christ came to raise us up out of the dust and sorrow," I countered. He was shocked and deeply troubled by the emotion in my singing. "Be careful," he advised me, "you may go too far." He had risen in the ranks of Mother Church and was secretary of our order in a short time. I had no such ambition. I loved working in the garden among the flowers and birds, and I sang my delight in life.

One night late, we were earnestly engaged in heated conversation. I would not abandon my new views on the state of humankind and the grace of God in the forms of love, and beauty, and joy. It was still and dark in his study; one or two candles burned without flickering, the light swallowed by the dark stone walls. He turned to me savagely and his voice echoed in the room, "This cannot be! You speak heresy! If you continue, I will report you to the church authorities! You are diseased and may infect our flock! I cannot allow it!" He turned his back to me,

"Leave me now. We will never speak again." *(Many years before this session, I had a glimpse of this scene, and the echoing of the abbot voice was the echoing off the cement block walls of my house, as a troubled friend raised his voice at me.)*

Shaken and drenched in fear, I left his room as he uncoiled the knotted rope to chastise himself. What was my joy in the face of torture, excommunication, and death? At dawn the next day, the sunrise shone on my huddled body, weeping in the garden. For a long time I did not sing, turning instead to copying the Bible on parchment and illuminating the letters with gifts from nature. I loved the patient work, and I especially loved one letter-picture that had a four-paned window looking out at foliage with a bird in the branches. While I had been painting this page, I had had many realizations: "To be happy is an internal thing; it doesn't matter what the outside of life is like. What is important is one's own soul; adversity teaches many lessons." The bird had told me that morning: "God's in his heaven; all's right with the world."

That was a deep revelation for me. Now I look at nature in order to illuminate the letters truly and perfectly. I study the leaves of the herbs and the ivy to show the perfection of the handiwork of God. I feel whole when I am in harmony with nature. The way the light comes through the stained-glass windows is like flower petals—petals which are only light and color.

In the garden, I still found my joy, but now it was quiet and inward. I remained apart from the congregation and most of the other brothers, preferring to keep silence and fast alone. *(I still have an internal war between being social and isolation—between community and retreat.)*

Eventually, my old ex-friend became a cardinal, though whenever we passed in the hall or during the service, he looked away. My wounds and fears healed and in time I went back to singing. I sang and felt natural like the birds that sing for joy and for the glory of God. I, too, sing for the glory of God. I also paint and copy the Bible for the glory of God.

For many long years my life was one of quiet, simple joy: the garden, music, writing, and illumination. The abbot became only thinner and more gaunt, and the fire that burned in his eyes seared all he chose to fix his gaze upon. He was consumed by his self-inflicted pain and suffering; and in the end, he became ill and wasted away.

When death was approaching, he called for me. It had been more than twenty years since we had last spoken. He said, "You may have chosen the better way. I have done all I could and more, and still I do not know Christ. He has eluded me. I have had no relief in this life, no joy, no peace." He paused, struggling inwardly, "and you seem serene. Whatever you found has sustained you through the years, but I have been consumed. I must ask you to forgive me for that night so long ago. And I ask you to sing the *Miserere* for me and pray for my soul when I am gone." His breath was labored as I took his hand and kissed it. Weeping, I agreed; and then the doctor shooed me out. At the door, I looked back. He was so thin that his body could hardly be discerned beneath the bedclothes, but he sighed deeply, "Thank you."

So, in the end, I sang my joy and love for my old friend. I lived on for many more years myself, growing frailer and yet rounder in the middle; studying, illuminating the Bible, working in the garden, and singing.

(Death) I am climbing up a ladder to get a book from a high top shelf. I fall and break things. I am in my room. I watch how light and color move across the walls of my little cell. There is a great deal of pain, but there is nothing to be done. Pain etched in colors. The corners of the room are filling up with angels. I am having a hard time. Then I slip into a coma. My soul rises up and two angels, one on each side of me hold my arms and give me a tug. There is a snapping sound and then I am free.

I stay in the room for awhile and watch the body as it sinks in upon itself. I watch, fascinated, until an angel tells me it is time to go. As I watch the body there is a life tableau; my whole life unrolled before me, but it was very quick and unclear. It flew past. Then it was given to me as a parchment scroll. I put the scroll under my arm and we go up. There are other monks waiting beyond the angels who came and did the work of freeing my soul. The monks want to take me to the next place. *(I feel uneasy about the monks, and would prefer to follow the angels, but there seems nothing I can do but go along.)*

I am holding a Pandora's box. In it are all my experiences of the plants, birds, and animals. I open the box and there is a most beautiful flowing out—a pouring out in ecstasy for joy of all the plants, animals, butterflies, colors, everything that I loved in nature. And they are all pouring out and expanding and dissolving in the etheric body of the earth. They are going home to their vibrational level of existence. And everything is very happy.

I look into the box and a few things have remained: a cat that had killed the birds I loved, and so I disliked him; a toad, and a scorpion. They are still at the bottom of the box. They were not able to fly free. The box shrinks down and I take along the small box with the things that I don't like. I ask, "What else do I need to take along?" My shadow steps out. He is all the negative things that I thought about myself. These thoughts and feelings did not hurt anyone else, but did me no good. The shadow is made up of the "sinfully depraved" desires of my youth, and all my negative thoughts about my natural beingness. So the shadow thing stands behind me to the left, which is the side on which I carry the scroll and the little box. That is all I can take.

Now we go forward. There are angels behind me to the right and left, and there are three monks ahead of me, leading the way. We come to the big gates. St. Peter is the "coat check" man. He says that not all of the things I have with me can go in, but that he has a place to keep them till I come back. I take the scroll with me and leave the box and the shadow. There is a large wall with cubbies where all the things are put. St. Peter rolls up my shadow and stuffs it and the box in a little cubby down low and left. There are all sorts of creepy, crawly things trying to get out of some of the other cubicles. Grey things and twisted arms and furry appendages are writhing around. "Good grief!"

I feel much better having parked my double/shadow and the other things that I didn't like in life. Now I can come forward to meet the Christ. Christ says, "You have been here before. We meet again." I say, "I want to understand some things." Christ says, "That's fine, all in good time."

Then the monks come again and lead me to a large ornate room where the pope is sitting. I climb up some wide red velvet stairs and I give him the scroll of my life. He looks at it, and checks it all out. Then he says, "You came pretty close to some dangerous stuff, very dangerous thoughts, my son, but you did not succumb so that's all right." And then he stamps my life scroll with wax and a huge golden seal. *(The power of the accumulated intention, thoughts, and rituals of an entity such as the Catholic Church or any large organization, can carve out a space for itself in the spiritual worlds. This was the pope's domain.)*

A couple of things happen here. If I had not had the thoughts that the church disapproved of, I would have gone to a big room that looks like the classical heaven to be put "on hold" in a nice way. People stay there, monks, and nuns, and pious others, until they want to do something else. Then the doors open to the rest of the spiritual world. Lots of them stay there for a long time. Some never come out. It is really a dead-end. *(There are many different regions in the spirit worlds that are created by concerted human activity, when the goal is to gain control over souls. There are a number of lodges and secret societies that engage in such activities.)*

(Past Life Review) But because I entertained heretical thoughts, I go to a "place" in kamaloca. There, I am escorted into a room with a table and a group composed of Christ in the center, and another brilliant being on either side. In their presence, I review the life just past. I see each tiny little moment when I could have done better. It was a life not of sins committed, but of gifts not given; sins of omission. I am smitten by the desire to make good and do better. I leave the "council table" and go to a room in which there is a living screen. There I spend time replaying scenes from my life that I would like to have done better. I can practice different approaches and responses and see which ones would work; see which actions or words are the best choice in each situation. It is like a second or third chance.

During this time, I also join with friends and family when I'm not working in the room on the past life. I learn many lessons: "I must be stronger in my beliefs." For example, in the confrontation with the cardinal, truth was on my side, and I could have persuaded him that we humans were really divine and not worms in the dust, if I had persevered. I capitulated too soon and too easily. Now I can duke it out with the cardinal, one more round in this place. We meet in a clear space, and there are angels and beings in the indistinct periphery. This time when I tell him what I think, I am so impassioned in what I say that he hears it. "Man is not just dust and sin, hateful in the eyes of God. We are part of creation. We are a wonder. Just as each leaf is a window into the spiritual world, and each bird a miracle, each human is divine and beloved of Christ." The cardinal is sad and crying because he rues his old life. We agree to do better next time around. We join with the other people of our karmic grouping, and we make plans for the next life-to-be. I want to be challenged, but I want the strength to meet the challenge this time. After the somewhat sedentary monastic life, I want physical challenges.

There are still some religious discussions, heated arguments really: shall we keep up with the Mother Church? Some say, "absolutely YES." Others have had it with the church and do not want to continue. We make a plan together, but now, I am not happy or joyful going into this next life. I feel a foreboding. I am not going with the Catholic Church, and there will be something to pay for that. There is a serious division in the group. We are standing in two different areas, waiting to go down to earth.

We then troop away to pick up the things we left in the cubbies. Now when I see my shadow, it is a small, tight, hard knot or seed, all compressed. I see it is the fruit of misunderstanding. That gets put inside me. Not in my heart, but close by it and it is a dark spot in my mind. A little etheric blight. Yuchk! Now the toad, scorpion, and shadow cat. These I must put in my pocket and take back down with me.

(Reincarnation) When my time comes to go back to earth, two angels come and lead me by the arms to the edge. The one on my left says, "You will not remember." The angel on the right says, "But you might if you really try." So I jump over the edge and slide down the ray of light (or tunnel) and "thunk" into my mother's body. It is cold and wet, and I feel, "Here we go again." I take the time to try to remember as much as I can while I am still in the womb, trying to imprint the memories of the spiritual world on the growing fetus; trying to remember the game plan for this life.

I am born a somber French boy, and have a reasonable childhood, but become an avid Huguenot, passionately against the Catholic Church, clandestinely teaching and preaching. I see how scars from the dogma of that last life left shadow thoughts in my mind, such as, "all that I think and feel is sin and depraved"; and how those thoughts poisoned me. In this life I meet a fine girl, but those guilty thoughts get in the way, and nothing happens. My adherence to the new faith results in torture and persecution, and I am a broken man. My beloved and I cannot relate, and so

I am not able to overcome the negative thoughts of the past and their effects.

I am tortured on the rack (in a civil, dispassionate manner), at the command of "D," who was the cardinal and abbot of the monastery in the past life, and who is again highly placed in the Catholic Church. *(I called "D" into this present life, even though he was the reason for the torture in that one. We must have made some progress, because things are not so bad in this present lifetime.)* The physical challenge leaves my body damaged, my heart wounded, and my mind slightly deranged. But I do not capitulate; or do I? I come out alive, although I am crippled and must walk with a cane. The light has gone out in my eyes; I am a walking dead man. I think that this physical challenge was a little more than I had bargained for.

The toad and scorpion are in my way all the time. I trip over them. They represent a threshold that I can't get over. In this life I have no real relationship with nature. I live in a cold European city, and hide in dark places. There is intrigue, tension, and fear, not a lot of nature like last time. At the end of this life, the box had dark trees in winter, and cold. Everything was very stark.

(Now I see that my childhood years in the wilderness in this present life have atoned for and balanced aspects of those two lives. My relationship to nature feels free, and I can see the Elementals. I may not need to carry anything in the box next time, because I see the beings working in nature and love them all. It just took a few lifetimes to get here.)

As we move closer to the present, the lives and afterlives seem to become more complicated. There are more karmic snarls to be unraveled and more intense psychological issues to deal with. At the same time, the evolution of consciousness has awakened capacities and deeper understandings, and human beings are forging spiritual tools for transformation.

CHAPTER 8

Esoteric Christianity

Evolution on earth can be described as the progressive materialization of the spiritual, cosmic, supersensible thoughts of the ground of creation, God. Everything is evolving, increasing in complexity and consciousness, or just plain changing. There is a pattern to earthly evolution. The "wheel of dharma" or the "wheel of life" is a great, huge, cosmic vortex. Everything within it is spiraling upward and recapitulating the old in new (and hopefully better) ways. The fundamental tension between unity and separation is infinitely elaborated as creation expands and contracts through rhythmic pulses between the two poles of every duality. There are fleeting moments of eternal cosmic balance midpoint, and 180 degree transitions at either extreme. Life fluctuates between evolution and involution.

Just as life is constantly changing, so death is also constantly changing. Neither side of existence, life nor death, is static. The whole cosmos is metamorphosing, evolving or devolving at all times. Just as life is different in each age or time period, each decade, century, or millennium, so the experiences of human souls are different in the successive journeys between lives.

As humanity has evolved over eons, charted by the rise and fall of successive civilizations, it has changed. Earlier humankind had other faculties and was more aware of the higher, divine beings. Humans interacted with their gods.

The myths and legends of all peoples hearken back to the time when plants, animals, and gods spoke to humans, and we listened and understood. As those faculties were eclipsed by dawning intellectual capabilities and materialistic exploration of the world, conditions changed in the death-worlds also.

We have moved into the twenty-first century, and humanity has now developed an intellectual, abstract, conceptual mind which is no longer satisfied with mere belief or tradition. Human beings are asking questions and seeking proof. Are there sufficient true stories, information, knowledge, and wisdom available to assuage the growing doubts and answer the piercing questions? And perhaps even more importantly, is there an experience available from which personal understanding can arise?

There are at least two answers to that last question: one answer is internally generated, and the other externally experienced. "Know thyself" has been a dictum of many ancient esoteric orders, and a time-honored pathway to wisdom. Reverence for the profound nature of humankind is a powerful force capable of awakening our spiritual sight. Enlightened self-consciousness is the goal of meditation, initiation, life, and death. The other answer comes from observation and research into the wonders and miracles of the material world. Both ways can lead to the spirit.

The course of evolution has been paralleled by a course of devolution: intellectually we have evolved; spiritually we have devolved. However, since the time of Golgotha, the turning point of time, we have begun to rise again spiritually. The overarching pattern of the earthly journey is to move out of the spiritual world, our original home, into matter; and then, after having understood ourselves in the physical world, to consciously ascend back into the spiritual realms, transforming matter into spirit as we go. The "deed of Christ" occurred at the deepest point of materialization, and is the decisive action that turned earthly evolution again toward conscious unity in the spiritual worlds. Christ came from higher planes than humankind, assumed human incarnation, and then went through physical death, resurrection, and ascension into the etheric realms of Earth.

Only three-dimensional human beings exist within limited time and are confined within spatial restrictions, and so, experience death. Beings of other planes or dimensions, such as angels and archangels, change and undergo transformation, but they need not die. Christ could only learn the lessons that death teaches and vanquish it, by incarnating as a human on earth where death is the only absolute. We human beings can learn the true significance of Christ's deed for life and death only here on earth, because it is here that death has its abode. There is no death in the spiritual worlds, but without the knowledge of Christ's experience of life and death on earth and the ramifications for future human development, the time between death and rebirth is incomplete.

The future of human evolution is intimately bound up with our planet's progression. Since our bodies consist of physical matter, which affords the spirit a vehicle on the three-dimensional plane, the vast changes in the earth's state of being and constitution (variously described in creation myths, religious literature, and now scientific research) have affected human evolution as well. It is also true that the evolution of each individual soul has consequences for the future of the earth, solar system, and cosmos. "As above, so below" and vice versa.

Our earthly knowledge, when supplemented by what we experience between death and a new birth, becomes cosmic wisdom. Earth as a being advances through successive embodiments, in conjunction with the results of human deeds, carried out together with higher beings.

From our actions we shape the part of the future for which we are responsible—our next earthly life. And collectively, humanity is responsible for shaping the next incarnation of the forthcoming universe. As human beings go through successive incarnations, so too, does the solar system evolve within the cosmos. The interplay of individual human and cosmic destinies is intertwined through consecutive lives and deaths. There is a mysterious connection between the cosmic planetary processes and the individual human being. As the earth's organ of self-consciousness, humankind is responsible for shaping her next embodiment.

It is difficult to be precise when referring to intangible, ineffable things that cannot be weighed and measured. It might be easier to paint about them, or sing, dance, gesture, or even telepathize; but words are the coin of the intellectual realm, so the task in our time is to translate the eternal divine into intelligent, understandable thoughts. Especially effective in that regard is the terminology of the western esoteric traditions Theosophy, Rosicrucianism, and specifically, Anthroposophy, the body of work developed by Rudolf Steiner (1861–1925). The Anthroposophical Society in America used the following passage to describe Steiner's work.

> In 1924, in Dornach, Switzerland, he (Steiner) founded the worldwide Anthroposophical Society for people who wanted to foster the life of the soul, both in the individual and in human society, on the basis of a true knowledge of the spiritual world. By devotedly cultivating his own soul life, Steiner achieved a clairvoyance that he could use to pursue spiritual research in fully awake consciousness. He pioneered the possibilities of treating spirit phenomena with

the same investigative seriousness that ordinary scientists bring to physical phenomena. . . . Emphasizing knowledge rather than faith, Anthroposophy gives a spirit-oriented understanding of the cosmos and what it means to be human. When human agency (anthropos) works with cosmic wisdom (Sophia), humanity can play its rightful part in the ongoing evolution of the world. Anthroposophy leads, in Steiner's world, from the spirit in the human being to the spirit in the universe.

However, independent of any society or culture, each individual should seek to actualize personal spiritual potential through his or her own inner guidance, following the promptings of a compassionate heart and clear, informed thinking.

Individual Human Development

Human permutation seems endless. Of all the billions of people on the planet, no two are exactly identical. Our complex DNA holds the promise of almost infinite variety. How have we arrived at this point—the year 2000-and-something? Perhaps, like Alice in Wonderland, we should begin at the beginning and go through to the end, which in a microcosmic scale, takes us to birth, and moves through seven year cycles to death.

The Threefold Activities of Humankind

1—Willing	2—Feeling	3—Thinking
Physical & Etheric	Astral	Ego/I

(1) _Willing._ Physical life as we know it begins at conception. A period of gestation within the mother follows for approximately nine months. During this time, the one-celled zygote (the product of the union of sperm and egg) appears to mimic the phylogenetic tree, from a one-celled amoeba through the successive stages of ever more complex forms of animal life. At one stage, the fetus, like a fish or amphibian, has organelles that appear to be similar to a tail and gills, which metamorphose as the process continues to move up the evolutionary scale of increasing specialization and complexity of cellular form and function. This whole astonishing process is captured in the phrase "ontogeny recapitulates phylogeny," meaning that the growth of an individual organism, from conception on, follows the same pattern of development as the evolution of that species. It is somewhere in the third or fourth week of this process that the spiritual Ego/I is joined to the physical matter of the developing fetus.

At the end of nine months, the biological evolutionary stream is basically completed, and a baby human being is poised to enter the world, and eventually assume responsibility for its own further development. The focus of a baby's growth, while continuing physically, opens to other aspects of intelligence, feeling, and soul.

The internal motivating self, the Ego/I, responds through the physical senses and body to the external world. From lifting the head, to crawling, standing, and finally to walking, the kinesthetic evolution of all life forms on earth is reenacted through orientation to the dimension of space. It is when a child walks that the physical body has achieved the first traditional milestone in physical evolution. The human being stands erect between ground and sky. This event foreshadows in physical form the ultimate objective of the human spirit, which is to bridge, in freedom, the heavenly and the earthly kingdoms.

Mastery of bodily functions is the motivating force during the next stage of growth and influences response to external stimuli. Throughout childhood, puberty, adolescence, maturation, old age, and unto death, the physical-material body is the medium of perception, the agency of response and action to the outside world. It is the *will* that is being trained, the connecting point between the visibly manifest physical body and the individual consciousness, which is unseen within. As we master the physical form in one lifetime, so the human spirit masters its existence through many lives. A single human life is as one step of the toddler.

(2) Feeling. During a human lifetime, other faculties are developing and evolving as well as the physical, and these unfold in seven-year cycles. The second body of experience that evolves through the life span is the emotional or astral body, which is hidden within the physical form. Babies begin expressing themselves by simple cries and coos. It is through emotive sound that the baby first expresses itself. Later, speaking develops out of the emotions. The feelings and emotions go through many stages and transformations. Just think of the infamous "terrible twos" of the toddler; the moody self-absorbed preadolescent; the volatile, rebellious teens; and all of the other emotionally-laden descriptions of the decades of our lives.

All these dramas are the result of the individual's expressing his or her needs, wants, likes, and dislikes. In the early years, these emotions take over the whole body; and preference, one way or another, is the ultimate goad to action. From temper tantrums, which may include floor pounding and kicking, to expressions of unrestrained joy and delight by dancing, clapping, and laughing out loud; from the blush of affection or embarrassment, to the blanching of fear, the body gives visible vent to the feelings.

It is through the emotions that relationships are formed among people. Part of growing up is learning to moderate and tame those raw emotions, and acquiring appropriate skills for their effective expression. It is hoped that age will bring maturity, peace, and a calm ripening of deeper human qualities and emotions such as perseverance, dilligence, equanimity, acceptance, and patience. As an individual can master these higher qualities of the soul, so too, in the larger scale of evolution, the human spirit masters qualities of itself, such as unconditional love and compassion.

(3) *Thinking.* The third facet of a person also goes through an evolution from birth to death: it is the intelligent thinking capacity of the mind. Whatever native intelligence a person has is neither obviously apparent nor able to be expressed by a baby. The mental capacity develops along with the physical and emotional bodies. The sense of self, the apprehension of oneself as an individual identity, is the hallmark of a resident thinking consciousness, an Ego/I. This conceptual faculty awakens and begins to express itself around the age of three, when children start referring to themselves as "I." Before that time, in and amongst the baby talk, they usually refer to themselves by name. Saying "I" indicates that the Ego is functioning and the child has developed a sense of itself as unique and separate from the rest of the world. It is the very beginning of the I/thou, self/other distinction. The Ego/I, the self-conscious, mentating entity has now incarnated another step deeper into the human condition.

A mature Ego/I is the first sign of consciousness of the spirit, and its current state denotes the level at which the whole of human evolution stands. Further stages of Ego/I evolution will elevate the soul to ever-increasing heights of clarity and consciousness until ultimately, we achieve Christed consciousness and are able, as He indicated, to do the works that He did, and more.

As we develop, the content of our thoughts is brought to us by life. Most of our thinking is rooted in the environmental world, and we passively receive impressions through our senses, which stimulate a series of associated thoughts. The individual exercise of personal will within one's thought process influences the quality of one's inner life. How we connect the thoughts; how we elaborate them inwardly; how we arrive at judgments and draw conclusions; how we orient ourselves in the life of thought; these qualities represent our inner destiny. It is through our thinking that we perceive the conceptual-spiritual world and beings, and specific cosmic verities such as math, logic, and philosophical truth. It is up to us whether our experiences are rich or meager. Our thinking creates the quality of our lives.

The Fourfold Bodies of Humankind

1 – Physical	2 – Etheric	3 – Astral	4 – Spirit Ego/I
Birth—7	7—14	14—21	21—28

(1) _Physical._ The physical body is shared with the mineral kingdom. Human beings use the material stuff of the mineral world to build up and maintain the visible body. The laws of the physical and chemical worlds apply to our physical bodies as to the rest of matter: gravity pulls it down, rain makes it wet. We get hot in the sun and cold in the snow. Strong acid would dissolve our bodies, and chemicals and drugs can affect all parts of us. What we cast off is composted back into the earth, as is our physical body at death. Hence the funerary proclamation, "from dust you came and to dust

you shall return." However, this injunction applies only to the mineral, physical body; for we humans are much more than just meat and bones.

(2) *Etheric.* The etheric or vital body is a collection of invisible life forces. Etheric forces, which enliven all plants, can be characterized as the upward rising force of levity; the inchoate urge to grow, proliferate, and metamorphose. In the human body, the etheric forces function to maintain cell metabolism and the processes regulated by the autonomic nervous system. These energies are charted on the meridians of Chinese acupuncture. During sleep, the etheric is still securely operating in the physical. The only time the etheric body withdraws from the physical body is at death. We share possession of etheric and physical bodies in common with the plant kingdom.

(3) *Astral.* The astral or emotional body is the home of the soul. It is another invisible part of us, which is sometimes seen clairvoyantly as colors extending beyond the periphery of the physical body, and is referred to as the "aura." The particular colors of the aura are a reflection of our feelings and our soul state. The astral body is centered in the heart and lungs, the rhythmic system, the organs most affected by emotions. Animals also have an astral body as well as a physical and etheric body, which explains their great loyalty and devotion, and their unbridled enthusiasm and joy: their primal emotions. We co-habit the astral realm with animals.

(4) *Ego/I.* The Ego/I is a human faculty that is undergoing intensive development at this time in evolution. A human being can say "I" only to indicate him—or herself individually. Humanity alone is self-conscious, and has developed the cerebral frontal lobes to think abstractly and conceptually. We each have an individualized Ego/I, and our development in this area accrues only to ourselves. This

Ego/I, this unique, thinking entity, is an individual spark of spiritual consciousness that is eternal. It goes through numerous incarnations, perfecting its lower vibrational vehicles (the astral, etheric, and physical) in successive lives through the ages.

Cosmic and Earthly Evolution

The Hindus and Buddhists say that all existence is made of the mind-stuff of the Creator; and our individual minds, our Ego/I's, are from that direct source. We are fragments of God working to become whole. From a Christian point of view, we are to become as Christ himself. What He did, we can and will do also. One of the most relevant aspects of His deed was to go through death consciously. Christ modeled lucid death.

As the ground-of-being, the Creator-God makes universes, galaxies, solar systems, planets, and all living creatures. As Christ, his son, is a divine being who focuses his creative powers on the evolution and destiny of humankind, so we are apprentice-creators and have our bodies and our planet to work with. Christ, the Solar Logos, came from the spiritual Sun to assist our evolution and create a path for us to follow. But in the mundane, exoteric world, that divine path is hard to find because of cultural bias from times past; very poor translations of the ancient texts; and the pressures and distractions of modern life; not to mention the forces opposed to human evolution. However, the esoteric, hidden, or occult explanation of the path, though complex, makes sense and can illuminate our journey through life and the afterlife, facilitating lucid death.

The big picture is huge, gargantuanly *huge*, but then so is everything, really. And the big picture is important, which is why we need quantum leaps and hundredth-monkey exponentials. This is where fractals come in, and nested Russian Matushka dolls, and Fibonacci spirals, and Pi; because actually, there is a comprehensible pattern (or series of patterns) that unfurl outward in infinite dimensions in all directions. This pattern is also cyclic; it contracts and expands, then contracts again, then expands again, infinitely. The basic premise is: "All is one; and then all is infinite variety, differentiation, and multiplicity; and then in the end, all is one again." Begin in one spot, cycle around whatever universe is handy and then return home wiser and more evolved for having taken the journey. All creation, humanity included, is playing that game. Once we were in the heart of the Creator, inseparable from the all-inclusive consciousness of God. This time is longingly referred to as "Eden." Now we are separate; we are each our own individual selves, learning by trial and error how to perfect wisdom from experience; and how to consciously return home to the Garden.

One physical human lifetime can be seen in this way. It begins from one cell, then grows to become a complete, autonomous, active, creative being; until in the end after death, the physical body is back to motes of dust or molecules of compost. The esoteric brotherhood of the Rosicrucians says that even the etheric and astral bodies reduce down to one last little atom, the seed atom of the heart. The Tibetan Buddhists refer to it as the "Indestructible Drop," a white and red drop in the heart the size of a mustard seed; so even the etheric and astral bodies display this rhythmic pattern of expansion and contraction. Daily life patterns are all in cycles, like the heartbeat, breathing in and out, and sleeping and waking.

What about the Ego/I? Consciousness is of the same nature as the ground of creation, the nature of God. Our Ego/I is the source and seat of our individualized spark of consciousness, our personal fragment of God. It is the Ego/I which cycles between merging into spiritual consciousness and separating into denser states of individualized manifestation and physically-bound consciousness. These differing states of human consciousness are experienced as the polarity between sleep and wakefulness, death and life.

The goal of the largest cycle of human existence, which stretches beyond our ability to reckon at this time, is continuing consciousness through it all: through life and death and into life again. Presently we have a degree of continuity between waking and sleeping, in that we remember who we were yesterday. We do not, however, usually remember who our spirit was in the previous incarnation. This characterizes the present state of humanity's spiritual evolution.

The universe and galaxies can be seen in this way, also. All over the sky there are star systems in varying stages of growth or decay. Some parts of the universe, so the astronomers say, are speeding away from one another; while others, like black holes, are pulling everything inside of themselves at speeds we mortals can't even imagine.

Consider our solar system, our largest human-scale venue. Whether we talk about people or planets, salmon or solar systems, we never return to exactly the same place, because in the intervening time spent traveling, everything has moved, transformed, and is different. We have gathered knowledge, distilled wisdom, matured, and learned a thing or two, so that we who are coming home are different also. Everything is different, but the pattern is the same. Returning home wiser is the goal of evolution.

It's a matter of scale. Our solar system is a unit of one and our earth is a unit of one, and each of us is also one.

> One heartbeat represents the same interplay of
> forces as there is to be found in a solar year. The

expansion phase is like the summer solstice and contraction correlates to the winter solstice. One human life in its entirety is the same as the Sun's going through the twelve signs of the Zodiac.[1]

As the human being develops in seven-year cycles, so there is a planetary cycle of seven stages of multiplication and differentiation. Seven cycles that last for millions of years, that we can be aware of. I'm quite sure that there is something before and after, but no human has been able to comprehend what that might be, so we will concentrate on the western esoteric tradition of the seven revolutions around the seven globes of the seven World Periods.

Seven Revolutions around the Seven Globes of the Seven World Periods adapted from Anthroposophy and Theosophy.

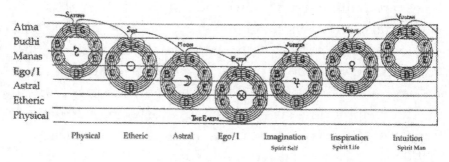

Our planet and solar system, themselves, have had long cycles of life and death, waking activity and then sleep (or *pralaya* as it is named in Sanskrit). We can begin to see the slow steady stroll of evolution. Our planet and solar system have gone through three full cosmic embodiments which all began in a relatively lower vibrational state than the preceding one. The first three revolutions of each World Period are devolutions into lower levels of materialization, which offer challenges and opportunities to all created beings to become conscious in relatively more difficult situations. One must learn to overcome problems by raising the energy level and evolving back to the higher states; to become a little bit wiser for having been around the galactic block three more times. At each stage it is not merely a perfecting of the capacities appropriate to that stage, but also of preparing the bodies (either planetary or human, depending upon which scale you are observing) for the next higher step in evolution as well.

To date, according to Rudolf Steiner, there have been three full World Periods of seven revolutions around seven globes each. We are in the fourth World Period, which is aptly named the Earth Period, and in the fourth globe, and through three and a half revolutions. We are at the lowest point of the whole multi-trillion year evolutionary extravaganza. It is a big picture, wheels within wheels spiraling down and up, and up and down. Just recently, we hit bottom; the lowest, densest point of materiality in evolution.

More specifically, 2000 years ago we "bottomed out," and were in danger of not making it back up again, until Christ came, heralded by angels and proclaimed by the stars and a few humans as the one to show the way back up. Christ not only *spoke* of the necessary changes and requisite states of mind; he also did it. He modeled the way. Because Christ is a cosmic evolutionary force who homeopathically affected all earth existence, his deed has cosmic ramifications. The mystery of Golgotha was the "turning point of time." He imprinted new patterns in the fundamental spiritual constitution of humanity, making possible the ultimate return. We are now at the farthest point on the periphery of expansion, so it's a long way home. The good news (sort of) is that it's all uphill from here. As some (infinitely human) body (Bob Dylan) once said, "been down so long, it looks like up to me."

What do we have to show for all our journeying? Well, we each have an individual physical body, and we each are raising the vibrational level of our specific bit of matter as we infuse it with love and consciousness. The emotions in our astral body affect and imprint the etheric and physical bodies, either elevating and enhancing the integrity of the physical matter of our bodies, or degrading it, depending on the vibrational level of the emotion. Positive emotions suffuse the physical body to the very marrow of the bones with life-supporting energy, healing, vibrations of integrity and wholeness, and unity with the cosmos (not to mention endorphins). Each human being is to become a free, conscious co-creator in the universe of his or her own body by understanding how thoughts and emotions affect the body and evolution. It happens anyway, and we either participate consciously and creatively, or not.

The evolution of our physical, etheric, and astral bodies is to be perfected into creatorhood by a process of transformation. The metamorphosis of the lower bodies can be described as "ascension"; that is, the growth and development from one stage to the next higher state. Christ's experience of death and resurrection was a map or template for ascension—the spiritualization and total metamorphosis of the physical, etheric, and astral bodies into the next higher dimensions of light and love. Ascension is not an automatic fact, any more than playing the violin beautifully is automatic for everyone. But there are means of learning to accomplish the next steps in human evolution, which will ultimately perfect consciousness and infuse the physical-mineral realm with love.

In our present time (the earth revolution of the earth globe in the fourth World Period), the incorporation of the Ego/I as the illuminating principle of the other three bodies is our immediate concern. The strengthening of the Ego/I is our main focus so that we can develop the consciousness capable of orchestrating the further evolutionary stages of ascension. There are future globes for the transformation of our astral body into the Spirit-Self level of consciousness, or in Sanskrit, *Manas*; the etheric body into Spirit-Life or *Budhi*; and the total transformation of the physical body into Spirit-Man or *Atma*. The ultimate goal is complete ascension into the next *pralaya*, the chaos of non-creation and resolution into perfect oneness with God and all creation.

Just as all creation and potential matter is the mind of God, so all the archetypes, templates, and patterns of manifestation are within the created bodies of higher beings. There is a hierarchy of existence from God down through many kinds of beings: Seraphim, Cherubim, Thrones, Kyriotetes, Exusiai, Dynamis, Archai, Archangels, Angels, Humans, Animals, Plants, Minerals, and Elemental Beings. Each kind of being is a helper to those below. In the Bible, the book of Genesis says we are the caretakers of animals, plants, and earth. A guardian angel guides the personal destiny of each human being.

> These future bodies (Spirit-Self, Life-Spirit, and Spirit-Man) exist as faculties of higher hierarchies who work on the rudimentary bodies of developing humanity. The organs and faculties of consciousness and perception are endowed to evolving humanity, like seeds planted in the earth by beings who have already gone through the particular stage, have mastered it, and are then able to plant the potential for future development into humanity. The image is a little like the precipitation of matter; crystals of salt, for example, from a completely transparent liquid. In this case it is the germs or

seeds of organs and potentials which precipitate from the surrounding spiritual world that is actually the spiritual substance and "bodies" of highly evolved, conscious beings. So, before precipitating into primal materialization or individuation, the physical, etheric, astral, and Ego of humankind were embedded in their divine origins and influenced the evolution of humanity from the cosmic spiritual worlds wherein the archetypes reside.[2]

After eons of separation from the Creator, the larger scales of evolution and ancient forms of existence are so foreign to our thinking, so abstract, that we can only vaguely conceptualize through analogy. But it is worth the effort to understand, because it sheds light on the how, where, when, and why; the meaning of life. And these have far-reaching effects on death as well.

In the first World Period, Old Saturn, part of the differentiated substance that was scheduled to become humanity achieved the rudiments of a physical body. We came into our primal relationship with the mineral world, which was just forming at that time, precipitating out of the cosmic soup of the last *pralaya*. The highest form of sentience was deep trance—a coma of unconscious universal cosmic consciousness, aware of gradations of warmth only.

In the second World Period, Old Sun, humanity received the beginnings of the etheric body, as well as a second edition of the physical body. Consciousness was similar to ordinary deep dreamless sleep, like plant sentience, which responds in a limited way to forces in the environment.

Then came the third World Period, Old Moon, in which the astral forces became active as humanity acquired a rudimentary astral body, as well as a second elaboration of the etheric, and a third development of the physical. The state of consciousness was like dream-filled sleep, a metaphoric picture-consciousness that presented symbols of external acts or situations. Those ancient dreams were creators of their own time/space, filled with images of floating color.

At the beginning of the fourth World Period, Earth, the first three globes were recapitulations of the first three World Periods, and humanity's physical, etheric, and astral bodies progressed a spiral higher with each revolution. Now in this fourth revolution of the fourth Earth globe, we have recapitulated the three World Periods in even smaller units, which are now humanly comprehensible.

We arrived at the time of which all creation stories speak. "In the beginning, God created the heaven and the earth," states the Bible in the first verse of the first chapter of the first book of Genesis, the foundation of Judaism, Christianity, and Islam. *The Kalevala*, the heroic epic of Finnish folktales tells of a great undifferentiated sea into which a celestial maiden fell from the sky. At long last a duck came and built a nest and laid her egg on the maiden's knee. When the maiden moved the egg was broken, but all was not lost. From the lower part of the shell was formed the earth; the upper part, the heavens, and the yolk became the radiant Sun; the white became the moon. Then all life began to spring up.

The epics of creation are similar the world over. All tell of the first recapitulation, the beginning of material existence, and how the earth was reconstituted or precipitated out of the amorphous void. The revolution which recapitulates the second World Period is always described as the coming and profusion of plants as manifestations of the living etheric forces. The third recapitulation of the developing astral forces took place on Lemuria, an ancient continent in the Pacific.

There humanity lived in a pristine state, merged in cosmic consciousness and in complete accord with universal laws. There was no individuality and no freedom; just infinite, heavenly harmony with cosmic evolution guided by beneficent hierarchies.

However, there were other experiences waiting beyond paradise into which humanity was catapulted by "the Fall," as it is called. Heaven is not a suitable environment for naughty, devolving consciousness, nor for developing self-consciousness, so we humans moved down a notch on the vibrational scale and became physically, materially incarnated.

> During the former Age of Pisces, in the Last Lemurian Period, the Ego/I of human beings individualized. It is allegorically called "The Fall" because it is a symbolic image of the descent of the spiritual faculty of consciousness into physical materiality. A spark of divine Ego (a tiny fragment of the mass of human ego potential) incarnated into an individualized form, and from this moment, is separated by matter from the totality of the universal consciousness. This brought the necessity of sleep for regeneration and remembrance; and death for returning from material bondage to the spiritual worlds; and for the progression of the evolution of consciousness, which is by nature, non-material.[3]

So there it is. If life is that way (and it is), then death is a necessary part of the equation so long as we are still involved in the material-mineral world. Our spiritual, non-physical, supersensible parts (our etheric and astral bodies and Ego/I) must return home often for rest and relief from physical limitation. The astral body needs daily relief and so we sleep. The etheric cannot remain separated from the spiritual for too many years, and so we die. The dropping away of the physical sheath frees the other bodies to return home to their respective realms.

The Fall was a major turning point in human evolution. Who was that red snake in the white garden? What was he doing there anyway? The Bible says that he was the fallen archangel Lucifer. Because he no longer could abide the gaze of God and had chosen to separate from the Prime Creator's evolutionary plan, he needed a new place for himself. So the newly formed earth was co-opted for Lucifer's intentions. Had Lucifer not arrived to tempt our progenitors, humanity would have ripened slowly in spiritual paradise; and when all faculties, organs, and abilities were sufficiently developed, we would have gently moved into further stages of physical manifestation in harmony with the divine plan, mature and well prepared for the vicissitudes of material existence. However, we descended into matter before we were ready. We were prematurely pulled from Eden (from paradise and union with the divine) without being prepared to handle the duality of the three-dimensional world.

Without the spiritual maturity to master the physical plane, humanity was thrown into an intense, steep learning curve that was activated by pain, suffering, and hard work, represented by the Biblical curse upon Adam and Eve. History is the saga of the ups and downs, successes and failures on our collective path of duality and of trying to get back to Eden and unity with spiritual consciousness. And more often than not, it seems, we got stuck in the negative painful pole, or tempted into extremes on either side.

As a result of that premature development, the reptilian brain and the autonomic nervous system were necessarily created and activated because we were not sufficiently developed for conscious awareness of our new environment. We had no self-conscious motivation or guidance, and needed an automatic response system for survival.

Because we came too soon to earth, we had not yet developed a clear consciousness, and a large part of our awareness was undeveloped, unavailable, sub—or unconscious. And it just so happens that Lucifer can live in unconscious states. Lucifer does not materialize physically, but mentally and emotionally. So a whole vast dark realm of human unconsciousness was created at the Fall, which resulted in a new residence for the fallen archangel Lucifer, and for his minions. The angels and the other hierarchies who are still in union with the Divine, do not have a subconscious. Their thinking, motives, and goals are as transparent as their bodies, and are at one with the divine mind of God.

This brings up the fact that the light of consciousness is the nemesis of the dark unconscious. Most psychological work and meditative practices aim at clearing up subconscious, buried information and experiences, and suffusing the dark unknown with the light of understanding and compassion. This is another reason why it might prove useful to understand death and transform the fear of it. Perhaps the reptilian "fight or flight" brain is ready for the evolutionary leap to the "Dragon Brain," transforming the image of the cold-blooded lizard devouring its own young to the fabled resplendent Dragon of wisdom, generosity, and power that soars between the worlds.

It is only at the beginning of that mythic time of earth evolution that we received the seed of the Ego/I. In this present revolution, the soul kernel is developing. The soul develops out of what we make of our emotions and the everyday human psychological aspect of our thinking. It is the sum of our emotional and mental responses to sense-generated life experiences.

There are three soul forces that will be developed in this Earth World Period. The first is the Sentient Soul, which began in the third Post-Atlantean epoch (4500 B.C.), whereby humanity experienced the presence of spiritual worlds in the physical. Through the Intellectual or Mind Soul, which began in the fourth Post-Atlantean epoch (1900 B.C.), the human capacity for individual thinking began to replace divine guidance. And finally, in our time, the Consciousness Soul began to develop in 1413 A.D. Now we must consciously look to the future rather than the past; our souls must become "apocalyptic." We must be able to esoterically lift the veils between the visible and the invisible worlds. Awareness must widen to include not only the physical world, but also spiritual and cosmic worlds as well.

In future evolution through the next three World Periods, humanity will not descend into physical material existence. Ascension will be an accomplished fact and higher faculties will develop. In the fifth World Period, called New Jupiter, our present astral body will be transformed into a new soul faculty of objective spiritual imagination, and we will have developed psychic consciousness, Spirit-Self. We will perceive waking picture-images and auras as a matter of course. There will be seven revolutions/recapitulations to perfect this new faculty, and then a night of *pralaya*.

The sixth period, New Venus, will bring the potential metamorphosis of the etheric body into soul-spiritual inspiration, known as Spirit-Life. As we become conscious of the inspiration from the spiritual worlds, we will develop the ability to look deeply into the nature of beings and objects, and to hear the sounds and tones emitted by each created thing. We will be able to perceive the sounds of the cosmos and dance to the music of the spheres.

Again will come a long *pralaya;* then in the seventh and final World Period, New Vulcan, we will achieve spiritual consciousness or intuition, Spirit-Man; this is described as an objective, individualized, universal consciousness that gives knowledge of the planet Earth in relation to the cosmos.

As a matter of scale, again, the single human life goes through a development analogous to the seven World Periods in seven year cycles:

Ages one to seven are devoted to building the physical body. This period concludes with losing the milk or baby teeth and the growth of the permanent teeth. It is an indication that the last vestiges of the infant body have been replaced and new capacities are anticipated.

Between seven and fourteen, the etheric body is the major focus of development. This is the heart of childhood; the mental capacities open, and learning takes place through all the senses.

At fourteen, the astral body begins its most intensive growth. This is heralded by the onset of puberty and sexual maturation. The emotions are often strong and volatile.

The age of twenty-one is commonly understood as the coming of age or majority. The individualized Ego/I now begins to express itself directly through the other bodies, and to integrate the total organism (body, soul, and mind.) The Ego/I is present and functional, and responsible for its thoughts and actions.

From age twenty-eight to thirty-five, the consciousness of the Imaginative Spirit-Self begins to accrue through the transformation of the astral body by moral thoughts and deeds, and altruistic emotions.

Thirty-five to forty-two is especially the time to transform the etheric body through pure, free thinking and meditative practices, into the faculty of the Inspired Life-Spirit.

And from forty-two to forty-nine, the changes in the physical body and the training of the will effect transformation into the Intuitive Spirit-Man.

There follow three more seven-year cycles influenced by the planets, Mars, Jupiter, and Saturn; and then the human being is free of evolutionary compulsion. Ideally, at the age of seventy, one begins to live freely, distilling the wisdom of a lifetime and starting the process of reverent preparation for death, which can easily take decades, if so destined.

Of course as we rise up the evolutionary ladder, one step per World Period, so do all other forms of existence. Angels move ahead of us to become Archangels, developing ever finer and more expansive abilities and bodies. The animals are hot on our heels, followed by the plants, aspiring to animal-hood, and minerals dreaming of growing, budding, and blossoming.

This exposition of the western esoteric worldview is held by Rosicrucians, Theosophists, Anthroposophists, and the odd science fiction writer. Proving anything of this magnitude is patently impossible. But these concepts, this overall plan of evolution for the whole of existence, and the successive steps in expanding human capacities and consciousness has been reported by contemporary mystics and clairvoyants, and can be found embedded in myths, legends, and religious scriptures, ancient and prophetic.

Some meditative and yogic practices allow a preview of potential states of future consciousness, and are designed to give an imaginative experience beyond the bounds of normal sensing, feeling, and thinking. Sense-free thinking is the least developed human faculty at this time. Pure abstract thoughts and concepts that are inspired by apprehension of the archetypal spiritual worlds are free deeds which are not karmically induced; instead, sense-free thinking is inspired by objective spiritual reality.

Even if there is no hard scientific proof (and there is none), an unbiased, clear-thinking, open-minded individual can see the logic in it. And that's good enough for me, because death has a context now. In light of this view of evolution, both life and death take on meaning and purpose; and can be understood, accepted, and indeed, prepared for and embraced as twin evolutionary forces operating in our greater earthly world period. And now we know—it is not forever. Things will change. Life will change. Death will change.

Reincarnation and karma are the modus operandi of human evolution. From a pragmatic point of view, one life is simply not enough time to experience the whole human condition. Death gives us an opportunity to learn what lies behind daily earth life. There is continuity and meaning to each action and thought, whether manifest here on earth or in the spirit-world beyond death. The divine soul matures in responsibility and evolves through the gifts of life and death, and life and death, and life and death, and on and on.

The propelling force of karma, the universal law of cause and effect, and resulting reincarnation carry the soul through life and death and into life again. Karma has two aspects. First, personal karma has to do with individual human relationships and one's own personal growth. Second, karma has a cosmic aspect, for we are all part of the human race, live on and have responsibility for earth; and we are dwellers in a solar system, a galaxy, and a universe.

The purpose of death is to continue the journey of the soul through the shadow side of life, in order to gain insights and lessons unavailable to a human being while engaged in the three-dimensional world. Human development has evolved by delving consciously into the physical world through progressively deeper materialistic thinking. The highly technical and mechanical world we live in is the result. But these material-scientific advances do not help the soul; other forces of mind and emotion must be developed for that. In the realm of death, the human soul becomes aware of the supersensible worlds, because the senses, which focus only on material reality, are laid aside; and the soul-spirit moves easily into formerly imperceptible worlds.

In life, we must acquire the knowledge and faculties needed to successfully complete death's tasks, which requires informed consciousness. We must gather spiritual knowledge and understanding of what lies beyond the threshold. The faculty of spiritual cognition can only be developed on earth; and even here, spiritual knowledge is an ever-changing thing. Since life and death are always evolving and moving forward into the future, no dogma, set of beliefs, or ritual can facilitate the union of divine and human consciousness for all time. It behooves one to continually seek authentic means of communion with the spiritual worlds, as well as to continue to plumb the depths of one's own inner being. Every age must come to terms with life and death relative to its own evolutionary stage.

In death, the individual Ego/I is freed from the limitations of matter to move into the higher supersensible worlds. The Ego/I learns lessons of transformation in the world beyond death; lessons that are not available on earth. Subsequent reincarnation is the opportunity, in a later more civilized (and one hopes, more evolved and progressive) time, and under new circumstances, to re-embody and continue transforming and elevating the physical, etheric, and astral realms.

Death is often pushed to the blackest recesses of the modern western mind; and from that vantage point it colors all choice, thought, and desire. It is time to stop denying death through fear and avoidance. Death has been waiting a long time for us to recognize its blessings and accept its gifts. Knowledge creates the light that dispels the dark unconscious, bringing value to the formerly lost and hidden, and instigating metamorphosis. Just as it is possible to awaken within a dream, and then consciously direct the dream creation (called "Lucid Dreaming"), we may do the same in death's domain. Lucid Death holds the promise of consciousness through the threshold and beyond; and upon returning to earth and remembering all that has occurred, the human being can infuse the new life with spiritual wisdom born of experience.

The analogy comparing life to death is far reaching. From birth to the grave, a human being goes through stages of development and a continuing process of maturation. Abilities manifest in an understood ongoing pattern. Babies learn to roll over, then sit, then stand and walk. They learn to speak and develop, over years, a more and more complicated vocabulary and the ability to express their ever more-complicated thoughts. Puberty arrives within a given time frame. The psychological passages of mid-life and aging are well documented.

It is similar in death. Each stage of the afterlife is a set of specific experiences governed by distinct cosmic laws. Particular experiences and qualities from earthly life are metamorphosed in each phase into spiritual skills and abilities for the next life.

The Journey of the Soul between Death and Rebirth

In light of this cosmic perspective, the journey of the soul beyond death takes a certain form, and there are specific reasons and explanations for occurrences there. All of the bodies (physical, etheric, astral, and Ego/I) are subject to the constraints of the physical world while alive on earth. At death these bodies are released and resolved consecutively into the laws of their individual vibratory realms, from the dense physical to the highest spiritual dimension of the Ego/I. There are nine steps or phases in the western esoteric paradigm: (1) Death, (2) Etheric Dissolution, (3) Kamaloca, (4) Lower Devachan, (5) Sun Sphere, (6) Higher Devachan, (7) The Midnight Hour of Existence, (8) Return, and (9) Reincarnation.

(1) Death is the doorway to the other dimensions. In the process, the spirit, astral, and etheric bodies are severed from the physical-material body which remains held by gravity in the three dimensional world. "Dust to dust, ashes to ashes"; the physical body is resolved over time to its constituent elements, which are recycled by the earth.

(2) Etheric Dissolution. The etheric body is now free to respond solely to the cosmic laws that govern the ethers: levity, warmth, flowing movement, expansion, proliferation, and metamorphosis, to name a few. Gravity no longer applies, and time and space are malleable. As the etheric body rises, disentangling itself from the organs and systems of the physical body, the etheric store of memories as a life tableau is transferred and imprinted on the astral body. Many people have experienced this life review or memory tableau because of trauma or near-death experiences. The phrase, "my life

flashed before my eyes" captures the feeling people have had in these critical moments facing death. Finally after about two to four days following death, the individual etheric body is dissolved into the etheric sphere of Earth.

(3) Kamaloca—The Moon Sphere. The following period of astral/emotional resolution is called kamaloca in Sanskrit, or purgatory, and lasts as long a time as one was asleep on earth. It is a replay of the unconscious dreams which reflect the daily experiences we had while awake. Basically, the time spent in kamaloca is a retrospective of life. Moving backward in sequence from effect to cause, the Ego/I not only observes, but experiences the results of its actions on earth. In experiencing both sides of one's actions (in life, the done deed; and in death, being the recipient of those deeds), one comes only at one's own hand to experience the results of karma. No one else is doing it to us. Now we are on the receiving end of what we have done to others. On earth we sow; in kamaloca we reap.

Nothing is lost in the spirit world. The review of the nights of the just-past life are also filled with the unconscious content that was not comprehended and transformed when we were living. The backward review does not stop at birth. During life, most impulses from former incarnations are not conscious, lurking in the personal subconscious and the collective unconscious. They manifest as instinctual, personally arbitrary likes, aversions, and unconscious impulses which follow us through each lifetime until we become cognizant of them and can choose our response. Becoming aware of all facets of our existence is the goal of conscious evolution. We have the opportunity of bringing the unconscious urges of past lives into full awareness each lifetime, healing and transforming them. If not, then they continue to influence our behavior, feeling and thoughts unconsciously. These are the chains of the past, rattling into the present time after time, life after life.

The spiritual practice of reviewing the day backward (called the *rückshau* in German) is helpful in resolving daily issues and concerns before they can be recorded in sleep. Becoming conscious of our errors and failings each day, and experiencing remorse at our flaws, mitigates the effects of karma in the afterlife. This is a relevant, conscious application of the law of karma, whereby we work to release emotional attachment and clear up misunderstandings while there is yet time on earth to atone and make amends.

Life goes on after death, but there is finality to many aspects of human relations. There are things we cannot change in the spirit world, but must passively experience in order to learn the full lesson implied by our actions on earth. The quality of our interpersonal relationships is one of these. Loving and respecting our fellow human beings develops a moral quality of soul, morality being an awareness of the inter-relatedness of all life and our inclusion in the family of humankind. After death, humans are drawn into relationships of "like-moraled" association. People who have made no attempt at intimate friendships on earth remain isolated in death. Friendship, love, and ideals continue unfolding in the spiritual world. Creating relationships while alive and manifesting karma on earth carries one forward beyond death.

Emotions arise from either the connection or separation with other souls. These feelings are a reflection of our own love or our own hatred on earth, and in the spiritual world we experience both intensely and directly, without the modulation of a physical body. A moral, spiritual attitude has positive effects; and immorality, defined here as non-love and disrespect for other human beings, has other effects.

> A person with a moral disposition of soul is able to preserve clear, radiant consciousness after death, whereas those with an immoral soul constitution sink into a kind of dim twilight consciousness (to which) the most terrible conditions of fear are connected. There is no greater fear after death than this darkening of consciousness.[4]

Since the time it takes for the astral body to be resolved is approximately one-third of the lifetime, a life of ninety years has a span of thirty earth years in kamaloca. During that time, the Ego/I is relatively close to the earth and it is possible for friends and family to communicate beyond death. Discarnate souls need information and understanding about the realms in which they find themselves. Reading to the dead in the western esoteric tradition is similar to the Tibetan Buddhist practice of reciting the *Bardo Thodrol* to the deceased. Spiritual information is necessary beyond the threshold of death, and sharing the wisdom we have acquired in life is appropriate and appreciated.

The sphere marked by the orbit of the moon is the outer boundary of kamaloca, and all vestiges of an individual's earthly, physical life and emotions are left there. The spiritual Ego/I must be free of earthly attachments to move into higher dimensions of clarity and pure consciousness.

The spiritual spheres of the planets and stars are the homes of supersensible beings. Those in the moon realm are intimately linked to the development of the earth. Highly evolved beings now reside in the moon sphere, who once in long-past history lived on the earth. They initiated humanity into the appropriate evolutionary stages of consciousness, and are known as the Seven Holy Rishis, and are the early gods and goddesses of the successive cultures that have spread across the world from East to West over eons of time. Now, their ranks also include the evolving Bodhisattvas and Saints. Angels and some Archangels have their spiritual home on the moon and descend to earth to assist in human evolution. Through the work of the moon dwellers, human actions are viewed in the light of cosmic wisdom.

> When we have passed through the gate of death and are together with them (the Angels), we must listen to all the Cosmos has to say about what we have thought, wished, felt, willed, and done on Earth. Our entire earthly life is exposed to the light of cosmic wisdom, and we learn the value our deeds have for the whole great universe. . . . [F]rom these lessons we develop the impulse to complete, to correct, or in some way to set right, during our next life on Earth, whatever we have done either to help or to hinder the evolution of the world.[5]

(4) _Lower Devachan._ The movement from the moon sphere gradually becomes a further radiating out into Lower Devachan or the Soul World. This realm expands through the inner planets Mercury and Venus where the Ego/I comes into contact with the supersensible beings (Archangels and Archai) who exist in those spheres. The planets are named for the Roman gods who are personifications of spiritual qualities. Humanity shares these qualities of the gods, and is influenced by their spiritual-planetary energies. Their names

and association to planetary bodies is a testament to the atavistic wisdom of ancient cultures, but it is not appropriate to make a direct correlation between the spiritual realms and the physical planets. The spiritual regions simply overlap the actual space bounded by the orbits of the planets in our solar system.

(4.a) Venus Sphere. Venus is the Roman name for the goddess of love, receptivity, and acceptance; love and nurturance are her gifts. This love applies not only to people, but extends to plants and animals, the whole Earth, and all creation. Unconditional Venusian love brings the spiritual Ego/I into relationship with others of like nature. For the morally aware, the social interactions now widen beyond personal, individual connections to include all others of a similar philosophy or religious belief, whether we know the others personally or not. Shared ideals create community in Venus' realm.

(4.b) Mercury Sphere. Mercury is associated with the mental faculties and intellectual ability. Experiences in the Mercury sphere differ according to the soul disposition. If the inner connection to all life has not been recognized, but has been blocked either through materialistic thinking or egotism, Mercury's sphere is barren. Dissociation from others during life leads to solitary confinement or isolation in Mercury. Those who are intelligently interested in others and therefore, socially inclined when alive, remain connected.

(5) Sun Sphere. The Sun is the heart of the solar system. It is the central light, heat, and energy source of our planet and the whole solar system. It shines without judgment. The Sun is the transition between Lower Devachan or the Soul World, comprising the inner planets Mercury and Venus; and Higher Devachan or the Spirit Land of the outer planets Mars, Jupiter, Saturn, and beyond. The Sun sphere is the home of the Christ,

who played a pivotal part in Earth evolution and continues to assist human development in death as well as in life.

At the time of the Fall, the premature descent into physical density, the angels and higher hierarchies instituted death of the physical as a balance and as an opportunity for further evolution. Had humanity retained immortality of the physical body, we would have been locked into that primitive stage of development only, and would not have progressed. Death made it possible to learn and evolve through successive lives in successive civilizations by accumulating wisdom and soul maturation.

For the mass of humanity in the fifth Post-Atlantean Epoch (the Greco-Roman age) the conditions after death made it difficult or impossible to reincarnate. During Hellenistic times, the saying "Better a beggar on earth than a king in the land of the Shades," expressed the prevailing view, because at that time, the soul was imprisoned in the house of Hades (lord of the underword) after death. Evolution was grinding to a halt, as the souls of the dead were trapped and immobilized by insurmountable karmic debt. The devolution of spiritual perception was causing havoc in Hell.

Personal karma can be atoned for in succeeding lives, but the karma of the collateral damage to others and society was becoming turgid. For example, if I kill you in one life, you can kill me in the next to balance the karmic scales. However, how can I, and then you, atone for the suffering and pain of our respective wives or husbands, and the loss of a father or mother to our children, or the loss of a member of the tribe, village or society? All these attendant karmas, the peripheral results of a single personal act, are metaphorically and biblically referred to as "the sins of the world." And by 2000 years ago, the enmeshed "sins of the world" of all the human lives since the Fall had made it very, very difficult for souls to reincarnate. Instead, they were trapped, caught in a web of unresolved negative karma. Human evolution was in danger of gridlock in Hell. Human consciousness after death had dropped to a dim shadowy reflection of the dim, dead, shadowy underworld of Hades.

An infusion of spiritual consciousness equal to the needs of struggling humanity was necessary, which is why Christ came to earth at that moment. Christ, the Solar Logos and Regent of the Sun, descended through the planetary spheres to incarnate as a human being. His mission was to free the imprisoned souls, and to create a new template for the journey after death for succeeding generations.

Now in the postmodern world, it is vitally important to remain conscious after death. The Ego/I must remain awake and alert to fully benefit from the after-death experiences. Since the successful completion of the Mystery of Golgotha, and the release of the trapped human souls from Death's clutches on Holy Saturday, Christ is now the Lord of Karma, "who takes away the sins of the world." He made lucid consciousness in the realm of death possible for all humanity.

There are consequences in death for remaining blind to spiritual realities, just as there are consequences for skipped stages of development in life. If nothing of a soul-spiritual nature has been developed during life on earth, then there is nothing to carry over into the spiritual world and the experiences in Kamaloca and Lower and Higher Devachan will be meager and shallow. The more we open ourselves to spiritual content in life, the better we fare after death. "Christed consciousness" makes it possible to remain awake through all the stages of death.

(6) _Higher Devachan._ Beyond the Sun, the purified Ego/I travels out to the planetary spheres of Mars, Jupiter, and

Saturn. There, it comes in contact with the archetypes which are the spiritual patterns for all species of life and all created existence; the idea or ideal which manifests in a million permutations.

> For everything natural on the earth, all living things, plants, rocks, minerals, there is an idea, an archetype in the spiritual world which may project itself on to the earth in a variety of different forms. . . . We meet the archetypes of the minerals, the stones, and the crystals (in the Mars region); the archetypes of all varieties of plants (in the Jupiter region); and the archetypes of the different species of animals (in the Saturn region)[6]

The experiences in Higher Devachan are more and more removed from earthly concepts. Language cannot convey the meaning of the spiritual worlds. Beyond the Sun, information and experiences are absorbed from the vibrational content of the higher realms. As Christ has been the guide up through the Sun sphere, clearing the past, now the redeemed Lucifer leads into the future. Lucifer, the fallen archangel, also has evolved through time; he now has a positive and meaningful relationship to the human beings who pass beyond the Sun. His function within the evolutionary scheme was also transformed by the Mystery of Golgotha.

(6.a) Mars Sphere. In the Mars sphere, the divine archetype of human speech is experienced. The spiritual evolution of Mars has been similar to that of Earth. Mars is the Roman god of courage and valor. However, devolution into aggression and violence continued on Mars until the seventeenth century (in earth-time). At that point, a spiritual being of a higher

vibration chose to ally his forces of peace and love with the Mars sphere.

Just as the process of the earth's evolution is a process of descent until the time of the Mystery of Golgotha, and of ascent from then onward, the other planets undergo evolution in a similar way as well.

> . . . [I]n the seventeenth century, the Buddha withdrew from earthly existence and accomplished for Mars a deed that . . . corresponded on Mars to the Mystery of Golgotha on earth. . . . [T]he Buddha became the redeemer, the savior of Mars. He was the individuality whose mission it was to inculcate peace and harmony into the aggressive nature of Mars. Since then, the Buddha impulse is to be found on Mars, as the Christ impulse is to be found on the earth. . . . It was Buddha's mission to exercise a pacifying influence on Mars.[7]

So now, when the spirit/I (the Ego/I totally purified by its journey through the Sun sphere) travels through the Mars sphere; the Mars experiences from the last life, can be uplifted to noble courage and transformed into nurturing, protecting peace and love through the "Deed of Buddha."

(6.b) Jupiter Sphere. As the spirit/I expands to the Jupiter realm, the harmony of the spheres becomes a grand symphony of tone filled with meaning. This music is the basis for the human faculty of thought.

> In the Jupiter sphere we encounter thoughts as living realities, not as pale abstract images, as human thoughts mostly are, but as thoughts of

the gods. The world of spirit is woven out of the substance of which human thought consists. Here (in Jupiter) we perceive the truths, the secret wisdom on which the universe is founded.[8]

(6.c) *Saturn Sphere.* In Saturn, the symphonic music of the spheres becomes a great choral composition of living meaning, for in the Saturn sphere complete conceptualization and comprehension fill the music with spiritual truth.

> Saturn, the last of the planetary spheres (remembered after death), is the great archivist of the universe. Here is the region of world-memory, where everything that ever happened still is. If we imagine the recording angels writing the deeds of men into their records, this is the "place" were those records are kept. . . . The fundamental fact of memory springs from this source.[9]

Saturn records the Akashic Chronicle (an etheric record of cosmic history), as well as the individual record for each human being's many lives. During the journey through Saturn, the spirit/I observes its own small part played in the galactic drama in the last lifetime. There we realize to what extent our past life was aligned with cosmic verities.

(7) _The Midnight Hour of Existence._ The journey through the outermost planets, into the constellations of the zodiac, and out into the galaxy is usually beyond the scope of human consciousness. Rudolf Steiner called expansion into the farthest realm of the stars "the midnight hour of existence" because the spirit/I is in a deep cosmic sleep. The divine

cosmic forces can then influence the spirit/I unhindered by individual consciousness. It has been my experience that we rest in the cosmic midnight at "Galactic Center" until we feel the call to return.

(8) *Return.* When we hear the call or feel the urge to return to earth, the spirit/I awakens and begins the descent back through the zodiac and the planets. The experiences we had in the planetary spheres on the way out, have now been transformed into capacities and abilities that we gather for the next life. The soul, full of karmic potential, then waits in the moon sphere until the precise moment for incarnation presents itself.

> Saturn gives one the germ of the faculty of human memory. Jupiter gives one the faculty to conceive human thoughts. Mars gives one the spiritual substance out of which the human ego proceeds. . . . At the same time in these three spheres the spiritual foundations of the future bodily structure are being laid (spirit germ.) . . . When one enters the Sun sphere again, the first feelings of gradual separation from the cosmos begin to appear. The heart in its spiritual aspect is formed here, at the heart of the universe. . . . In this realm, too, one makes the first connection with the hereditary stream in which, possibly centuries later, one will be born. . . . In the spheres of Venus and Mercury the shaping of future destiny proceeds in relation to the particular family and particular nation to which one will later belong. . . . [W]ith the entry into the moon sphere, decisive steps toward being born take

place. . . . [N]ow it is the task of spiritual beings to dim down the consciousness to the level of the dream consciousness of a little child.[10]

(9) _Re-incarnation._ The process of descending into reincarnation is a long and complex process, as the Ego/I moves again down through the planetary spheres. The results of previous karma are bestowed upon the returning Ego/I, which then incorporates the effects into the new life as abilities and potentials. The strength and clarity of forces experienced in the world of death affect the new physical, etheric, and astral bodies in the coming new life.

> When the spirit-germ (spiritual forces that create the physical body, the personal archetype) has at last descended to the parents at the end of its long journey down from the spiritual world—the spirit 'I' itself, still in the spiritual world, gathers ether around itself there, and for a short time becomes a being of Ego, astral body and etheric body, the ether having been drawn together from the world-ether. It is not until after conception, during the third or fourth week of the embryonic period, that the human being unites with the organism that has been formed by combining the spirit-germ with the physical germ, and bestows upon it the etheric body drawn from the world-ether. One then becomes a Being composed of a physical body, an etheric body drawn together in the last moments . . . and the astral body and Ego which have gone through the life between death and rebirth.[11]

(9.a) Birth. The astrological birth chart is a diagram of the karmic relationships designed by the spiritual beings of the planets and stars from the karma of the last life. The planets are so aligned as to mirror the karmic abilities and difficulties which are then impressed into the etheric body of the baby as it draws its first breath.

Our individually created karma is the mechanism for fulfilling our destiny. Destiny and karma are not immutable laws of imposed predestination. The living human being has the opportunity to exercise free will in response to the events which are karmically ordered. Most of the events and relationships in our lives are set in place and motion by past karma, but in our response to these predestined life situations, we exercise our free will.

We can also develop our cognitive capacities and so alter the consequences of karmic encounters. When we meditate or pray, we are free; when we love and appreciate nature in any of its forms, from gardening to stargazing, we pursue the path of free will. The decision to discipline ourselves; to learn new skills and tools for self-awareness; to intend and persevere in awakening and strengthening our inner faculties, and accomplishing outer deeds of love and compassion; all these are choices that transform karma and create new destiny. These are the contemporary steps of modern initiation and conscious evolution.

The conceptual matrix or cognitive womb that has been described in this chapter will help one to understand the images presented from direct observation of the life after death in the following journeys. The cosmology of Rudolf Steiner is the most complete that I have found, and is a large enough picture to encompass everything that has presented itself so far. I have given only a terse description of the salient points of his worldview, and only as they apply to my particular theme, Lucid Death. There are hundreds of Steiner's lecture cycles, and many books, to which I would refer my gentle readers.

Spiritual Regression: *Nobleman John in England in the Late 1500s and a Nameless Child*

The following story of the author's is set in England, south of London, not far from the White Cliffs of Dover in the late 1500s and into the 1600s, when humanity had begun to develop greater capacities of soul and thought. The consciousness soul faculties were awakening at this time. This story clearly describes many of the features of the contemporary journey after death. The italic insertions in the text below refer to the specific stage of the western esoteric journey after death and to explanatory comments.

(The induction led down a winding stairway into a room with three doors. When I entered the room, I realized that it was a massive stone basement beneath a medieval fortress.) The stone stairs beyond the middle door led upward to the bed chamber of John in the castle in England sometime in the 1600s. The bed is huge and canopied; I, John, am dying of some lung disease or poisoning. My second wife and my three sons are here, as well as a priest and a doctor. My daughter does not want to attend because she is afraid, and my death is rather gruesome. I am terrified and not ready to go, so I struggle and thrash.

In a word, I have been "despicable" during this lifetime, and I have no real belief or hope for heaven or peace. My sons can hardly wait for me to die so that they can grab the power, the money, and the castle. My wife sits stony-faced and will be glad when this mess is over and I am gone. "Hurry up!" she is thinking.

(Death) I can't let go, and struggle until exhausted. In the dying light, I catch a glimpse of my long-dead Grandmother, the only person who really loved me and was kind to me in this miserable life. Once I see her, I know everything will be all right, and I release and cross over to the other side. In my grandmother's presence, I feel again like a loved child. She is so sweet and loving, but she feels sorry for what I had become in my later years. She and I go to a quiet place to wait until all the family and friends from the last lifetime come together again in this new spiritual world.

(Life Review) While we wait, I see my whole life enacted below and at a distance, so that the images are small and symbolic, or stylized. I simultaneously know why I had done what I had done. For Instance, the harshness of my Father when I was little had stopped parts of me from developing. It was as though pieces of my soul and potential were broken off of the functioning me. Those parts of me that had never been able to live had been waiting for their chance, and concurrently now, with the replay of my life, those separated aspects of my self begin to live also. Every choice and crossroad of my life is now lived from both sides. My Grandmother and I, John, watch a number of possible lives unfold, while in the midst of it all, I follow the thread of the actual lifetime. I understand how and why I made my choices. As a child, many parts of my self were chosen out of anger and hurt, and I see what happened and how those early painful decisions set a pattern.

And now at the time when relationships with women entered my experience, I see how I chose to be unkind. I was bitter and harsh just like my father, instead of kind and beautiful. And when my own children came into the world, I see how uncaring I was. I am sorry now, and I see that they are right to gloat over my death, although I'm sad for them because those negative feelings won't do them any good in the long run; and I see how my unkindness is generating more unkindness.

When I was young, my guardian angel was with me all the time, but I did not listen. Sadly, I see that when my guardian devil appeared, I did listen. *(Each human being has a guardian angel, and since the Fall, has also a personal imp or devil.)* There was a definitive experience as a child that broke the connection with my angel. My father did something cruel and violent to my mother and grandmother, and they disappeared from my life, leaving me with no feminine relationships. A large part of me died then, too.

We have been looking over alternative lives for a long time. Grandmother is tirelessly supporting me in finding the pathways of love and joy, and in seeing how this just-past life could have been better. We are waiting for the others to arrive and gather together, but they are all looking over their lives as well. Finally, I feel finished and ready for a change. Grandmother asks, "How do you want it to be now?" I say, "I want to dance and be happy and to feel love." Pictures of laughing children and merry waltzing wives swirl though the old castle. But that is not to be.

(Kamaloca—Moon Sphere) Instead, Grandmother and I find ourselves in a green place in nature, having glided here on thought. We are meeting with others to decide how it will be, and what we would like. I don't really know what this means, but I am eager to find out. We all, and now "we" is a larger number, stand around a large table with paper and pens and ink. I am not able to focus too concretely, so I can only say that there are about a dozen people gathered. We are wearing the clothes of our past life-time, which are elaborate suits with ruffles and neck pieces and hats and wigs. The women have tight fitting bodices and large cumbersome skirts, and none of us are very comfortable. We are properly dressed for court in a cold climate, and here the air is perfectly warm. At first, I thought that I was going to design and oversee the building of a huge castle, because I thought that was what I wanted now, but it seems foolish to build a fortress in this beautiful, peaceful place. So we are all wondering what we

would really like. What is essential? What is worth doing here, worth creating?

We speak, but the real communication is telepathic because we all hear and understand one another effortlessly. We decide that we will build a pavilion, open and airy, and that we will wear long nightshirt-like gowns because they are so loose and mobile, yet cover the body. We share a feeling of comfort, support, and excited communal energy, and it feels good. We all seem to be about the same age. We have bonds among us, but not individual relationships at this time and place; and we honor everyone's contribution to the planning sessions as we figure out what we want to include in our new world.

Each one of us had experienced religious feelings on earth and we all want that devotional feeling again, so we create a "church" consisting only of gorgeous colored windows and organ music. I love being in this environment, and feel rejuvenated as I pray on my knees, bathed in the intense colors. Although time is different, I think that we all live here for quite a while. As each part of our world is decided and created, beings from higher realms come to teach us regarding the meaning behind what we wanted. We are always learning about the cosmic laws of how and why the universe functions, and our part in the unfolding of the larger destiny of earth and humankind.

We are all overjoyed by what we have created and wonder how we can bring these feelings and ideas down to earth when we incarnate again together. Some of us want to go to earth right away, and others feel that we need more time and tools to be able to do so effectively. For the first time we seem to have a choice. One of the wise teacher-beings suggests that we "go on," and we all feel the rightness of this thought. But before we "go on," there is a surprise in store for us. We are graduating from kamaloca. There is a celebration with lots of others joining, congratulating us, praising our work here in this world, and encouraging us to "get more tools" and then accomplish our goal of bringing love and cooperation and understanding down to earth. Everyone here works for that ideal.

(Lower Devachan—Venus Sphere) Everything becomes black but bright for a time as we travel, gliding at lightning speed through space. The next environment we find ourselves in is not a visual place, but a soft pink directionless fog. It is a "feeling" realm. I am alone now for the first time, but I feel secure and know that I will connect with my "family" again. Now I experience my life replayed again, but this time I am aware of the force of love as it blossoms and then is squashed by life circumstances. The thread of "love" goes in fits and starts in my whole early life, and then gets to a place where it is squeezed and confined. The ribbon of "love" is reduced to a tattered thread; broken, with whole sections seemingly missing. I can hardly breathe, the realization of the lovelessness of my old life is so painful. As I watch, at my death, I am released and love floods into my whole being.

Now I relive my life again as it could have been if I had been filled with love. I am almost swept away by the intensity of the blast of love that sweeps over me and I see dimly through love-glazed eyes, that love could have burned through everything, made all my earthly experiences almost divine. If only I had known love then! Here in this place, love is perceived almost as a substance, a palpable material from another world, which is tremendously powerful, stronger than anything on earth and more valuable than gold. By "grace," it pervades all existence. It is always there, always available. Human beings must simply stay open to receive it. Yes, that is the trick: to know how to open to love. It is pretty clear that I did not have a clue in the last lifetime, and it makes me sad to see how loveless, lonely, and powerless I really was. We are gifted with this force of love according to our life experiences and how we learn to accept. The cosmic "pool" of love is infinite. We are given as much as we can take.

In this realm, then, the soul views its love experiences three times over. The first is a replay of the love relationships of the past life. The second replay shows the individual soul how the past life could have been if love had been ever-present. The third replay I like the best, because the "family" is reunited. We play the old life out moment by moment, but this time suffused with our new appreciation for the power of love. Every experience we recreate together is soaked in love and it cleans everything. All the old memories are washed away in the tide of love. Now we are experiencing human love, human interrelations based on love; like holding the babies, being held and hugged and kissed, being appreciated and adored.

We stay in this bliss for a long time, even after our old life is finished. When we make this love feeling, the ambiance is pink with rosy highlights and even red points of passion, but as we merge deeper into the feelings they become lighter and lighter and more intense, as though burning away the dross of that old life. When it gets to be a total white heat, the purest that love can be, in that moment we are shot out of this world like a seed from a pod, ejected out into another bright black space and on our way to another realm.

(Lower Devachan—Mercury Sphere) In this next realm or state of consciousness, we receive wings. It is like being an "angel." The environment is similar to the beautiful church we built in our first coming together. There are only glorious colored windows and radiant light, peace, and divine music. We fly in and out of the colors playing harps and singing. Then, I begin to hear the voice of "God," a deep, rich voice pronouncing words carefully and lovingly: love, peace, joy, industry, harmony, and so forth. As each word is spoken, I feel the glory of its reality. I am filled with the understanding of the highest possible meaning and import of each word. The ecstatic presence of each word resonates inside of me like a living experience.

In time, the nature of the words begins to change, and now I begin to *see* the words enacting their full meaning rather than experiencing them inside myself: anger, shadow, imposter, lies, fear, and so forth. I am grateful that I can see them and not experience them, since it would be terrifying to have them live within me. From a distant state of equanimity, I see these terrible words as fallen parts of the beautiful first-spoken ones. I observe them as loveless human attempts at fulfilling innocent needs and longings; states of being which consciousness has not penetrated with its warm light of knowing and accepting.

"Why am I being shown this?" I ask, and the answer awakens within my soul, "So I will understand, truly comprehend the reality behind words, and know that there is life and meaning in everything." We have choices as to what words we will fill ourselves and our lives with. And I know that this place may be "hell" for some people, should they choose to live into the negative shadow words and reject love even here. Everyone has an individual experience. There is little chance for choice here because mostly the words come to us by way of karma. On earth we create "heaven" or "hell" by our choices there, too.

My group has chosen to go on now, to singing and making music. Because we now all know what the words really mean and that they have power to create experiences and inner states, we sing with a new purpose. We sing songs raising fear up into peace, or bringing the shadow into the light. Our music helps the unhappy and degenerate concepts.

It takes a while because words that are not imbued with beauty, truth, or nobility must be reclaimed and filled with love and satisfaction, and that task takes time. As we work, each soul learns how to transform realities. When that is done, and the whole world in which we are is radiant and bright, we have risen like a sunrise up to where it is just a step into the next realm.

(Sun Sphere—Transition) We walk up vast gold, gold, golden stairs into infinitely huge beings of golden splendor whose bodies and consciousness *are* this world. We are in the living being of the Sun. "Where is Christ?" I ask, and the answer reverberates throughout the golden air, "The tomb is empty! He is not here." I realize that Christ is on Earth, or more truly, He is in the etheric everywhere, and yet I feel a pang of disappointment at not finding Him. But my sorrow is minuscule and soon melted away in the golden splendid beauty of this place. The lesson here is to learn of immortality, to come to *know* that I am a ray of the Creator, and to experience reunion and going home.

My perceptions have expanded so that I have a universal perspective and I can see from the far distances of space, as well as experience my soul-self in the Sun. I see a band of light going out from the Sun to the center of the universe where the Creator is. But really, of course, the ray of light originates from God. I soar on that ray up into the outer planets. I approach each planet from beneath, circle the equator, then fly up to the north pole, and zoom down into the center of the planet.

(Higher Devachan—Mars Sphere) I remember only a red blur as Mars.

(Higher Devachan—Jupiter Sphere) Jupiter, which I experienced most strongly, was rich purple, and the great halls inside the spiritual body of the planet were filled with long sustained chords played on an organ or many organs. I felt that I related to some being here especially, but cannot bring it into consciousness.

(Higher Devachan—Saturn Sphere) Saturn was a deep bluish color with a somber, intense feeling. Inside was a world of bustling activity, large halls, and other smaller, more intimate spaces.

(Outer Planets—Uranus) Uranus was very much smaller, and the whole planet, inside and out, was a luminous iridescent, multi-colored silver.

(Out into the Stars towards the Midnight Hour of Existence)
The universe is filled with highways of light on which souls
from all galaxies and systems travel when "going home" to
the center of creation. Now it is my time to journey forth. "I"
still feel like "we," although I am no longer specifically aware
of who the others are. So we travel out into the far reaches
of existence. I know that we can, and sometimes we do, stop
along the way in the signs of the zodiac. There are so many
worlds and systems that support life, perhaps not as we know it
on earth, but *consciousness* which manifests in myriad diverse
forms where souls can learn lessons not available on their own
home planet.

As I left Uranus I began to sing, "home, home, home, I'm
going home," as I headed out even farther away *(up and toward
the left)* from earth. I arrived home at the center of the Galaxy
with a gesture like turning inside out. I soared up and around and
down and inside out, so my spine was all curled up inside of me.
I am no longer the soaring golden cross-like, Christ-like human
shape, but have now metamorphosed into what looks like an
individual egg in a mass of "frog-eggs." This whole environment
is a soft mush like a gelatinous mass of soft little spheres, and
in the colored center of each one is a point of consciousness.
It feels like we are rubbing our tummies together because we
are all turned inside out, and we are bathed in a kind of radiant
purple glow. This is a place of unity; we are all "one" here, all
connected, yet each point of consciousness is still self-aware. It
is the gestation place of souls.

I sleep in unity in the heart of Galactic Center, until I hear
faintly that I am being called. Something or someone is calling
me from far, far away, and I rise up from my egg and pop out at
the periphery of the mass, like a bubble bursting; and I see that
all around human beings are popping out of the "unity-eggs," as
they hear the call back to earth, too. I realize that it is the other

human beings that I created future lives with who are the ones calling me to gather again and return to earth.

(Return from the Stars to the Solar System and the Planets) On our way back from Galactic Center, we function in some way through the universe. We are energy particles or rays or beams, an enlivening force streaming through space. As I follow the call to return to the reassembling group, I stop again through the planets. I feel jubilant, and report in each planetary great hall that I am on a mission back to earth. I feel very different, incredibly vital and energetic. I am not the person that I was in the last lifetime. I am progressively becoming who I will be.

(Return to the Moon) As we come closer to our own solar system, I begin to see things more clearly until once again, we find ourselves in our white tunics back at the drawing board, the planning table where the family first met after our last earthly death. Now we are radiant with new knowledge and enthusiastic for our next adventure. Who will we be? What will we do and how will we do it? There are so many choices, so many possibilities, and so many alternatives.

The family settles down to creating new lives, knowing that it won't be just grace and fun. It has to do with the "words" that we brought back with us. We must choose to design lives that will align with the higher meanings of the words, and transform them into material, physical life. We must learn to heal the concepts on earth, as we experienced in the "colored window" sphere.

(Reincarnation) We all sit around and run scenarios of how our future lives could be. There are thousands of things to decide to do. Once it is agreed upon, one by one we incarnate again. I knew that my main lesson was to experience the love on earth that I had felt in the spiritual worlds. I came back as a little boy who did not live very long, only a year and a bit more. I was loved and adored by my parents who felt deep compassion for my frailty and the suffering I endured from the illness which

took my young life. I felt so much love that even the pain was worth it.

This journey was the most complete in regard to the realms beyond the Sun. Again, it is a challenge to translate supersensible experiences into understandable sense-based forms that can be communicated to other people. So much of the actual experience is just feeling, color, or energy. And "out there" are so many other sensations for which we on earth have no name.

CHAPTER 9

Glimpses Beyond The Threshold

The varieties of life after death are as diverse as life on earth. Each experience is absolutely unique, although similar patterns are apparent. Our interpretations of after-death experiences are colored, modified, and inflected by our belief systems. To a large extent, what we think and believe about the spiritual world is what we see there, because in the spiritual world *thought* is the densest substance, and is immediately creative. In that world, there are no inviolable physical laws for solidity. The mutability of the mind is the most stable human element in the spiritual worlds. There is no "one way" to cross the threshold through death and to journey toward reincarnation. Personal karma, destiny, time, culture, and belief all affect the soul's experience.

This chapter consists of bits and pieces from many spiritual regression sessions. Each is a little glimpse into a particular aspect of the after-death journey. The individual travelers use their own words to express their experiences, so each fragment has a unique "feeling" generated by the particular vocabulary. Some of the longer, more conceptual pieces are further elaborations of my own personal journeys. I have traveled extensively in those other worlds and have communicated with many kinds of beings, and so can follow a more intellectually conceptual track once the past life has been explored. And I am often prepared with a question or two.

Most of the descriptions of beings, places, and activities from the spiritual regression journeys I have facilitated, are located in kamaloca, the moon sphere. People's remembered experiences are centered here because this realm is most similar to earth conditions. Lower and Higher Devachan and everything out beyond the Sun are completely different, and we have few words or concepts to describe situations there. The stories of kamaloca, however, are rich in detail and immediately comprehensible to an open earthly mind.

After one particular journey it was suggested that a little more information would be appreciated:

Then I found myself before an angelic "scribe" who sat at a desk with a huge book. The scribe read:

There is a general pattern to the afterlife journey and most souls do experience the general pattern to some degree. The beginning and the ending sequences, just after death and before birth, are cloaked in the cultural metaphor of the past and future lives.

How far a soul travels out into the deep spiritual world is a result of that soul's evolutionary development. The phases and steps that were observed in the last session are just one possible path. This or any particular, specific journey is not 100% of the whole journey; each is a personal variation of the many possible after-death experiences.

In the spirit worlds, time is variable; therefore humans of different levels of development can go through different processes after death and still return together for the next life.

The Christ has many names and figures, culturally and worldwide. Anyone who knows love and kindness and who lives by the qualities of the Christ, however He is named, can take the whole journey after death.

In another session, the subject of the changes in religion was broached. The past life just explored was set in ancient India, and after reviewing the life, death, and afterlife, we asked the participating deities about the changes over the millennia.

I ask the goddess how it is now when a human crosses the threshold. In the present stream of things, what happens? And I see that the general pattern includes a life review which occurs from whatever level was important to the person. Then the whole cultural karmic aspect is included, which in the ancient experience was speaking to others, hearing what others spoke about oneself, and feeling their thoughts and opinions.

But now there is at least one more level. That is, if someone has had a philosophical background that is wider than this religious view, then those concepts need to be resolved in a different way. The religious view, which in ancient times everyone accepted, took care of the resolution, the transformation of the very innocent evolutionary stage of direct belief and experience of the gods, because the gods were present and accessible to humans at that time. Now, if one is a Hindu, one's religion takes care of only a small part of the complex life of today. All the psychology, complications of life desires, and relationships with mechanical things; these all need to be resolved in a different framework, because the Hindu religion does not, in a sense, cover those aspects. Now, a person goes to other realms, where these other issues are under the guidance and aegis of other beings.

In the present time, there are choices or options having to do with the inner connection each person has made with the spiritual worlds. Some people have gurus, who help with their development. Or sometimes gurus hold development back, because they can gain more power in the spiritual world if they control the energy of other souls.

I see highly evolved people, the epitome of "human being-ness," like Gandhi, who guide some people. These highly realized people might be an evolution of the seven Holy Rishis, or they may be archetypal human beings who personify one aspect of human potential. They are beings who help people resolve a particular aspect of themselves beyond the threshold.

It is difficult to say what the karma of a mental pursuit is. Intellectual people are influenced by souls like Francis Bacon (thirteenth century philosopher) and by the Arabic influence from the Persian school of Gondishapur, which flourished in late antiquity. These intellectually oriented souls, institutions and thought processes affect the afterlife of many people, just as they do on earth.

Karma usually results from interactions between human beings. The pursuit of mathematics or philosophy or inventions does not have the same kind of karma as the more mundane or personal aspects of human life. These intellectual areas of human endeavor are guided by archetypal human beings who help in the transformation and resolution of abstract concepts.

The Christian impulse blends aspects both of the gods and the archetypal human being, because Christ was not just a religious figure, but an evolutionary force. He is not just human, but has to do with higher hierarchies and higher beings of a divine nature. That is why Christ can help in the whole afterlife. Christ is now the Lord of Karma and the transformer of all qualities and properties as well. That's why Christianity can influence the other major religion's afterdeath at the present time.

One of the most beautiful and highly evolved experiences in kamaloca occurs when people of different religious beliefs have come together during life. Then, in the after-death, there is a bridging of differences and becoming one. A unifying force, a unifying principle, lifts everyone up together. When living people on earth form friendships with true communication; when they allow true expression of their differences and their different ways; and when they can hear and accept each other; that creates a really beautiful thing in the spiritual world after death. That creates a little place of freedom, a clear place of transparency, with no color and no influences upon it. Just a very clear place in which the people who are involved can experience freedom and non-compulsion on any level. That is rare and incredibly appreciated, because so much of what we do and experience (almost everything, actually) is under the compulsion of karma on one level or another.

Assisting at the threshold is an important job, and some newly deceased souls stay close to the gateway of death for awhile to work together with the angelic helpers who are always there to greet specific people when they die. Nowadays there are many newly-dead souls that need extra help because of the disorientation from traumatic deaths.

There are helpers who orient new souls to the new level and help them process the last life. They are on another dimension, not earth and not physical, but just as real. Here they are much more aware how thoughts affect self and others.

135

When you first come and pop through the bubble, there are throngs and throngs milling about and welcoming one another, contacting, connecting. You can stay there welcoming others or you can move into a garden area with a few hundred related light-bodies. There is a vast area above our heads, but we don't go there. There is more than one garden area and other lines you can go and stand in. I don't know how it works. But everything feels totally correct and right. Once you burst through the bubble, all is secure and nice and everything is okay.

I'm an adult now, not a girl any more, here in the spirit. There are helpers here. They greeted us and then came with us. A lady is holding my hand and we are here amid rolling hills like on earth, and there is lots of water. There are buildings here with rooms, many rooms. People I knew before I went to the earth are here. The people in this place are all healers. They help those who have just died and there are so incredibly many of them because of the epidemic, but now the plague is over. This is our new home. Our purpose is to help people on earth and other planets. We send them energy. Some of the people here help those who die to go to the first place, the grassy flower garden. I'm still adjusting and healing myself. I haven't started working yet.

I have been here for some time, and now I am sending energy to the earth and the people on the earth. The plague was created. Many of us went to earth to heal the things that were happening in the early 1600s. Our presence did help and the plague allowed many of us to leave when our tasks were complete.

The essence of all kamaloca-purgatory experiences is the resolution of the astral body, the clearing of all emotional attachments. This can take many forms, from fun and games, to serious communicating, to isolation and pain. The quality of the experience is the result of the individual's karma, and most souls agree even to the painful experiences because they know that the only way to move on is to more through everything that stands before one.

Now it is time to move on to another place which is higher up. It is a field of enactment. My husband from that last life is here now, but I don't really want to come anywhere near him. I don't want to get close, and I don't have to. But I can say and speak anything and everything I ever wanted to say to him now. It is like I am raining arrows and spears and darts at him, and he is being tormented by all the things I hurl towards him. He is being pricked and pierced and darted everywhere. And I am protected from his retaliation.

I speak to everyone who has been in my life. And if I say kind things then they feel warmth and love and nice feelings, like I'm saying to my mother and my father who were very sweet. And to the Brahman scribe, there are some things that I say. "I do love you, and I wanted our souls to have more of a relationship and connection." And also I tell him how betrayed I felt by him. I say, "I had hoped that our friendship would be stronger, but I understand, and I don't hold anything against you. I know that you were afraid, and felt powerless." These are my longings and they are causing him a searing pain, a singeing heat.

As I speak to these people from my life, they experience what I say to them in a total bodily way. They feel the feelings I felt in life, that they themselves had caused. Everyone is aware that I, Nataranja, am the one who is sending these feeling experiences their way, and that they have been receiving the truth from me.

So after I have finished speaking, it is my turn to be in the receiving place. Although my husband shouts lots of things at me, I don't feel them because they are not true. When some things are said, I do feel them, but only if the statement and feeling is true. From the Brahman, I feel so much conflict, hot and cold together. It is a tormented feeling, and I understand that my mere existence caused him torment, a mixture of desire and repulsion, passion and fear. I feel what those feelings were for him because they are true feelings, not just anger or stupidity, like the barrage from my husband.

I feel complete and empty after I have said everything to the people in my life, because I have given them everything that I had felt and carried over into this plane. In that way, I made space to receive from them, and now at the end, I have experienced my last life from both give and take.

❧

I am moving out of the body. I feel relief, motion, and freedom. I sense a presence: Shankara. He is very big, wearing a blue robe, and I have a sense of welcome. I know him. He is a teacher for me in the spiritual worlds. I have a feeling of failure for this life, so his welcome is very important. Shankara goes with me and we sit at the edge of a garden on benches and talk. He asks me about the last life and I tell him it feels like a waste because there was great promise and potential that went nowhere. He tells me it wasn't my best but not the worst either, and I have a glimpse of a vast span of time and it seems less significant. I leave Shankara and walk in the garden alone. Later perhaps, I will look at the other lifetimes and get the larger perspective.

Now it is time to review what really happened in the last life. Shankara comes with me to a rectangular hall with a boomerang-shaped table. He sits at one end and four other beings are there. I stand in the middle. I am asked if I'm ready to review the life and when I say "yes," I turn and face the visual experience behind me and we all watch it. I feel detached and puzzled as to the purpose of the life and they say, "trial run," meaning it was a practice in pieces, a rehearsing; a rehearsal of risk-taking and stepping out. I just didn't have the strength and faith to see it through, to be patient. It was a confrontation with fear and discouragement and they won. But it seems to be okay. They ask what I might have done differently, and I say, "Reach out and look around." Self-absorption happened and I forgot to look up and out at the world. I forgot who I was.

♰

I don't really join a group but have a one-on-one conversation with an equal light-being and we communicate what it is we want in the next life. We communicate that we both want to learn a lot; in the last life I couldn't really perceive anything, so I want to perceive everything. He wants that as well. He wants to learn a lot about being human, how to overcome difficulties, and to know how to be caring instead of having to be cared for.

♰

A lot of the light bodies up here are familiar. There are a couple of hundred beings in this group. They come and go a-flowing. I'm resting in a garden place, and some of the other beings are clumping together. Now there is a group of ten people. A reddish being comes and communicates that we are a connected group, and that on the planet we will have relationships, and we need to be aware of that. We will be there for each other's learning experiences. Our little clump is rather rambunctious and our destiny is to bring positivity.

♰

I am here with one other being and we are designing the next life. I'm surprised it's going to be so quick. We draw, creating a weaving of people and themes. I have an opportunity to see what some of the challenges might be: 1) Pride: it's a long process of dissolving the ego, dissolving the identification with the lower ego. 2) Invasions: I always have a timetable, and am controlling things and invading others. So I ask for help. "Where can I turn, because I didn't have much help in the last life?" I have to open my eyes to see. There are some threads to follow:

—I cannot direct and control life this time.

—Open and surrender.

—Trust and be patient.

—It was all here before you began.

—Remember that nothing is as it seems.

The beings of the afterlife exist in non-material dimensions and often appear only as light or energy. Different kinds of beings have different forms. Some are dressed in cultural clothing, some only in color or light, and some are experienced only as a kinesthetically felt presence.

The beings all look the same. They are dressed in their light-bodies. Some are brighter and have white light streaming from their hearts. Some lights are more muddied. There are taller more pinkish-red ones, and the main one tells everyone where to go. The taller reddish or bluer ones come and communicate to groups which form around them.

There are beings here that are wearing brilliantly colored gold-embroidered saris, and the fabric floats up and becomes wings. They have gorgeous wings, sari colored wings of rose, red, emerald-green, and deep-sea blue flecked with gold. They float horizontally. They are tending to people like me.

I go up to the stars, and small children with wings take me into space, into silver, blue and golden light. I am going toward the Sun.

I turned up, and went into blinding white light. The light melted into liquid gold and then Christ could be seen in the golden glory. As I approached, He stood with His arms outstretched like the cross, and we merged and He imprinted His likeness into my substance. I said, "This is what I am and what I will become. Christ in me, and may He fill my spirit. Not I, but Christ in me." I became a miniature golden Christ-like figure, with outstretched arms and began to soar up into the heavens above.

There are many different kinds of environments in the spiritual worlds: natural, architectural, and symbolic.

There is a fountain in the center of the garden. I am drawn to it. I catch the water as it falls, wash my face, and pour it over my head. It is cleansing, and helps me remember. It helps me release the old, past lifetime and reclaim myself as soul.

I went into a soft pink place, very billowy or feathery. After being there for a while, I perceived shafts of different colors that were in patterns as though they shone through a stained glass window. Each color has a different sound, and I am permeated by the music and color of each one. The yellow sang the songs of Hildegard von Bingen in a woman's high and pure voice. The blue sounded like a magnificent, melancholy cello; the red was trumpets. I experienced each one and then I began to twirl and whirl among all the colors and heard a beautiful cacophony of music. I asked for understanding, and received that each sound washed some aspect of the senses clean from the last life, and impressed and refreshed the senses with the archetypal truth of their being. Color and sound are actual healing *forces* in the spiritual world.

❧

I am on a path through living green grass, very short and brilliant. I see a bridge in the distance and a white city that sparkles far, far away.

❧

We are in an open temple with no roof, and columns open to the sky and stars; or maybe it's a memory of stars. I sense gold, white, and blue.

❧

I saw the tapestry of life, and the warp is the continuum of human challenges (virtues and strengths to be won), and the weft is woven of the actual activities of our lives, which is why there are sometimes big karmic snarls on the loom of life and uneven

142

stitches, and dropped and unraveling threads. But as I looked into the future I saw the possibility of a smooth and beautiful weaving of the tapestry of life.

After the library, there are many alternatives. I go to a place like an amphitheater filled with old friends. I know them all, whether personally or because they are famous: Shakespeare and Monet, artists, actors; people from throughout all times. Actually I don't know what I am doing here but it is an honor because they are so great. It's like a reunion. The people like me here, are those who have been touched by the great ones' lives, through their work or shared experiences.

The library or house of the Akashic Chronicle is often visited to review aspects of the past life or to learn of options for the future.

Floating upward into the light, I am very sad because I did not want to leave, but my body would not sustain me any longer. A man in white, Ho-ola comes to me. I have known him since before; maybe I have always known him. He is more familiar than even my mother. He doesn't have to use words; I feel his love in my heart. It's a knowing. Ho-ola takes me to the library where that life is recorded along with all the other lives and learnings. Everything past and future is here. Ho-ola and I are looking at who I am, which is many things: mother, father, baby, teacher, student, artist, thinker, feeler, and Ho-ola is a part of me too. Ho-ola and I became one. The part of me that now is experiencing my particular life has separated again. I was all the life experiences that Ho-ola was the keeper of, and now I am once again a fragment, a part of that wholeness.

Once the souls settle into the environment of the spiritual world, they may choose to become involved in many enjoyable activities and exchanges.

Now I am in a place with very green grass where everyone is wearing white. I am strolling alone. I come upon an old friend. He is acting like a pirate (swaggering around) but that's not who he really is. He is reminding me of his last life journey, a life that he experienced with me. That is why he still has the residue of the rough and boisterous pirate energy. He is teasing me and wants to "get my goat" because he was a grand pirate and I was "only" a mother and a wife. He is so comical, a complete caricature, so I also see the humor in it and we laugh and laugh.

I am with a group of other beings. We put our hands into the center of the circle and it makes a star and all the energy runs through my body.

I spend time in classes, sometimes inside, sometimes outside, and with different groups of people. One favorite class is sitting in a circle by the gardens and playing a game called "Forgetting and Remembering." We pretend to lose ourselves in a dense cloud and then follow a thread to find our way out again. We are creating and connecting the threads. It's amazing; when we come out, we all laugh because we can't believe we felt so lost. We practice a lot.

I gather with the others, friends and family and fellow soul travelers. We play a game about how we might be in the next life-to-come. We act out scenes and imagine out our lives together. I want to be challenged but I want the strength to meet the challenge this time. When we have worked out our ideas, we bring them to a panel of higher beings and they chart our scenarios for the next two or three lifetimes. Our plans are then inserted into the timeline of existence.

Although we incarnate in diverse cultures, places and times, it may be possible that we have created our own genetic base by reincarnating within our own family lines in the last few centuries. We may very well be our own ancestors. The following journey of a woman with Native American heritage in her ancestry illustrates this fact.

I chose a Native American family for the next incarnation because part of my purpose is to help heal the conflict between whites and Indians. I chose Indian because they have the most agony and resentment, because the whites had slain many of their people and separated and hurt others. This has created a very big wound that must be healed on this planet. My task is to help heal the wounds of both Indian and white man—to help them all realize that they are all human. I will become a guide. It was a hard life, days of little to eat. We broke ground, we trapped, and we led people across the mountains. It was a good life with a lot

145

of love and caring. Our conflicts were with the elements and lack of food, and the red man and the white man. I am the red woman and I am married to a white man who respects and honors the laws of my people. He is a brother to my people. Emma is one of our descendants. She is her own great-great-grandmother.

The briefest of encounters on earth (such as a miscarriage) can result in a spiritual connection, and the souls involved can continue to work together beyond death.

I go up and up and things are lighter and lighter here in the spiritual world. I'm glowing a lot and there are a lot of glowing ones here. I see my parents and they are brilliant too. A little being comes toward me and says that he is my unborn son from the complications of the pregnancy that ended in a miscarriage. We really like each other, so we work together and look after my wife who would have been his mother. We send her a lot of love.

Ghosts or earth-bound souls are humans that have not left the immediate earthly etheric plane for kamaloca. The ties to the physical are sometimes difficult to break, and there are unfinished lessons that can keep a soul attached to the material plane. Usually, as soon as the souls are clearly aware that they are indeed dead, and as soon as their concerns are addressed and resolved, they are relieved and happy to move on.

In the next example, a woman had a twin in the womb who was very weak and who died soon after birth. She was never told about this tragedy. She never knew consciously that she was a twin, so she had experienced a life of inexplicable emotions of unworthiness because of the intrauterine and birth trauma. After her death, she was told about the absent twin. She chose to linger in her old house for a time, in order to process the information while still on earth, before transitioning. Had her still-living son or his wife been able to see her, she would have appeared as a "ghost," as those souls who linger are called.

I'm dying in the house. My son is leaning over the bed with a look of pleading because of his sadness at my not loving him for who he is. We are all victims of something we do not understand. I want to reach out to him and open my heart to him, but I can't. My son is holding my hand and crying. His wife is just looking on; she doesn't expect anything. He wants me to tell him that he is good enough. But I can't tell him—not to be mean; I just can't.

It is finished now, and I am looking down on my body. My son and his wife and the doctor are there too. My son is so sad, like a little boy longing for the mother who was never there for him. My spirit feels heavy and sad for him.

The weight of my sorrow is holding me here. My spirit is sitting down at the drawing room table. I am wearing a high collared blouse and a big skirt. God, a wise old man wearing a hat with a feather, comes and sits beside me. He is telling my spirit about my twin baby brother in our mother's womb. I felt that something was wrong all my life, but I never knew what it was, so I felt as though I had done something terribly wrong. It was all subconscious, and so it affected everything in my life for the worse. I never gave myself the right to have what somebody else couldn't have. When the twin baby wasn't making it, and I felt that in the womb, I made myself bad and shut down my feelings so as not to be conscious of my badness. I didn't feel that I deserved

147

any of my parents' gifts because he, my missing twin, didn't live to have any. I didn't feel worthy of anything even nice.

My spirit twin is here now, and I am spending time with him and feeling the love from long ago. We are still in the drawing room talking. The clothes are only a reference point; otherwise, I am just a huge sheet of energy; we are sheets of energy. Finally it is time to go. Now my spirit twin and I are walking in the gardens of the spiritual world, talking and holding hands.

War seems so tragic, stupid, and useless from my personal point of view. But perhaps on the global scale, or on galactic charts, there are reasonable reasons for war. Is it, perhaps, the perfect opportunity to test our commitment to light and peace, and hone our skills for transmuting negative energy?

And then the sword of war cut us apart and asunder. Violent, insanely cruel events tore our lives and dreams to shreds. The seamless web of unfolding karma was snarled and knotted in clots of hideous torture, unspeakable agony, and fathomless despair. The machinations of war pulverized our hopes and ground my body to black blood and dust. There was no moment even for good-bye. My family and I were taken away; and later, far, far away and beyond caring, I died a humiliating, pitiful death in the concentration camp with hundreds of thousands of others.

The turmoil due to war scrambled the destiny trajectories of many people. Because it was a time of war, lots of people had brief intense "make-up" lives for balancing the past, in short intense experiences. The lives terminated by war are for cleaning up karma so that the souls can come back more peaceful and take on the task of making the world a better place. Lots of negative karma is burned out, and people appear more innocent. Those dying young return with extra energy for the next life and usually, a commitment to do better.

By becoming more awake and conscious in our daily lives, it is possible to make better choices, and to initiate better thoughts, actions, and behaviors in our own personal lives and collectively in the world. Perhaps the need for war will be superseded by the conscious choice to evolve positively. As my mother says, "Sweetheart, just remember, what you don't choose to do out of love and freedom, you will probably have to do, anyway, though pain, suffering, and sorrow. So just do what you know is best right away." Perhaps we should mind our good mothers and there will be no need for war on this planet.

The relationship of the living and the dead is very real and effective when people are aware of the continued connection beyond death. Those who have died often remain close to earth to comfort and assist those left behind; we, the living, can experience them and work together.

As soon as his soul leaves the earth, he moves to a place where loved ones from that life (deceased mother and father and older brother) are waiting, as well as guides and other discarnate loved ones. He chooses to stay between life and death, and watch over his wife, Isabelle, and their children until she joins him. Many humans choose to stay between the worlds and share with others who are still alive. He watches over his family and is a spirit guide. He shares in dreams, and sometimes in waking moments, as much as possible, and whenever his family will think of him in a calm and receptive way.

Separation is an illusion; souls are always connected. The individual soul accepts the delusion of separation by setting the spirit world apart from the physical. We can break the delusion by just being with the so-called-dead in the imagination. That's why, when people die, the spirit says "remember me." Think of them; that's how you can stay connected. The imagination is real. It makes their spirit happy and allows communication. It makes the energy denser and brings them into this reality. It's all spirit, whether living or dead. Thinking of them "thickens up" the energy. The molecules of thought call them to you; imagination thickens the energy and draws them to you. It creates an energetic magnet. This works for angels and guides too.

When his wife dies, he is there to greet her, and she joins him. Hand in hand they say goodbye to their children then they move on, to integrate with their higher selves.

The time is coming when living people will "midwife" the dying over the threshold, to see that their souls are received into the light and company of angels and loved ones on the other side. The following describes an example, which arose spontaneously in a hypnotherapy session.

> We are both in bed and she is holding me and I'm holding her; and then I slowly leave my body. It feels like she is right there holding my hand. Marie actually does go with me a little way when I die, and she makes sure I am okay. We rise up and look down on our house and there is light shining through where Anna and the kids are; we go up and it gets smaller and smaller like we are going into outer space. I see the world getting smaller and smaller behind me. Things are getting lighter and lighter, and then Marie gives me a hug and she goes down again, and I wave and keep going up into the light.

The dead have access to the Akashic Chronicle, records of spiritual truths, the evolution of human civilization and consciousness, and glimpses into the future, which we on earth do not have. Many take on tasks to create a better future for all humanity in the sciences, the social sphere, and in nature herself.

> There are many in my home group (about a hundred) that I work with, know, and have close ties with and great love for. We gather together because the power of healing is much stronger in a group process than as individuals. This work is a mental process. We work in a large beautiful dome where we gather and use our mental capacities to send healing light, love, and creative energy where it is needed. We work with healers in physical form on many planets including Earth. We send them energy, and they have the ability to accept it; it flows through them. We have several teachers on earth who use our work. Very few things are

created on earth; they are created in other dimensions and then given to the few who can receive and use the information. In our future lives, we will personally use our own material that we created in the spirit world in the past.

⌖

I went to a place were work was being done to prepare people to be born on earth again. We are healers, and I am among those at the threshold of incarnation, and we are specialized in science. The earth is getting ready for the arrival of the technological age. I will be born in 1823 again, to help change the energies on the earth and prepare humanity and the earth for new technology. I will help prepare the people and earth to receive technology that was given by the spiritual scientists themselves. We, including the scientists, healers, philosophers, and the keepers of all other forms of knowledge cannot share with a planet until the energies are right. The people have to be ready for change. Humans tend to resist change unless something opens them up. We cannot force even good technology on humanity unless they are in a state of willing reception. Healing and working with energies is just not as simple as healing a wound. It's a change of spirit on a local and worldwide level.

⌖

The movement through the threshold of death was easy, and Nathan was back into a place he knew well. He works with the elements of nature on a higher level and he loves his work. The elements of nature (plants and even Earth herself) take on physical form but are still connected to "All That Is" through the level where he does his work. He works with the energies, and the process of flowing from pure energy to the life forms that live in plant, animal, and mineral, on this planet and others also. Everything that occurs on the planet, including humans, is created from the energy of "All That Is". The energy mutates, or is "stepped down" through the vibratory levels to become manifest. Without this process, nothing would exist in this world. There are many, many who work like this with nature!

Nathan and five other people are in a place of light green trees and bushes. They were creating plants which disappear and then they make more. A succession of energy is flowing into Nathan's world and then flowing out into other worlds. With his mind and the minds of others, he creates plants of energy, and then sends them down to earth as seed life.

Since the soul after death takes flight out through the planetary spheres and far out into the cosmos to the midnight hour of existence in Galactic Center, it is understandable that some memories of other galaxies might emerge. The following excerpt, experienced in Higher Devachan, describes a soul group with origins in another star system.

I move on to a new place, a new gathering and this is more like home. These are beings that have been traveling and exploring many different parts of the universe and come together periodically to remember who we/they are. Here I am not young. I have been on the earth for some time, but not forever. I came to learn and explore from the Pleiades. I see different beautiful crystalline dimensions. It is so strange to have been starting the earthly journey as a young soul, but still being an old cosmic soul. It seems that I don't always get to reconnect with these other travelers after each life, just periodically for recharging.

This galactic group takes some time revisiting our original intentions: to serve the raising of consciousness and the coming home of consciousness. Whatever we do for ourselves is for the purpose of coming home to the source of all. There is a call, "Come home"; and when I hear the call, I am home. There is no lack, no looking for anyone. I am absolutely full and overflowing. It is as if we are not separated; to call it "love" doesn't really do it justice. So we affirm and remember what "going home" feels like so we can recognize it when we are in another life.

When the last details of the life-to-come are completed, there is often a pause before the next incarnation, as the planets move into the perfect position for birth. This next excerpt describes a soul-blending just prior to the descent.

When Marie dies, she just flies up and lands near me where I have been waiting since I died, and I am so excited. Marie and I (James) are going together on the journey. We are inseparable; we go everywhere up and down levels, and we explore like we did when we were alive. Sometimes our unborn son, who we lost in a miscarriage, is with us; he has a lot of stuff that he is doing. We do a lot of creating and experimenting. We do things with our hands (spinning and weaving glowing, golden light) and now we are doing it together. Amidst the spinning and weaving, a little gold being pops up between us. We are weaving ourselves into one being. We are creating one thing out of the two of us. It says, "I am all of you." The little glowing being will go on and continue for both of us, and we are going to stay here. It is a new soul. We don't want to go back to earth as individuals again.

The little glowing being is going to be born. It is a new soul, but it is both of us and it is eternal. Marie and James are there and say, "Be One." That's part of the challenge: being one from two. So, wow! The little being is born and it's me; and I'm a Gemini, which represents both James and Marie. Being a Gemini is easy because James and Marie were so much a part of one another. Their love is important to bring to earth again and I can do so by acknowledging and loving myself and sharing it and being an example of that, and recognizing that I am what they are sending on.

There is always time for celebration.

And then there is a big feast with all the gods and goddesses, or the good ones at least, and lots and lots of people. We are drinking the draught of forgetfulness. We are celebrating what we have done. We have finished certain things here: we have seen our old karma, we have experienced the results of it, we have chosen what the new path will be, and we are celebrating the fact that we have done all this. We are enjoying the beauty of all this gladness. There is dancing and the music is fabulous. It is so beautiful, even the elephants are dancing.

Each person is honored here. At some moment, each person stands up and is acknowledged and honored and one or another of the gods or goddesses says something to them because the person is under their wing, their protection. Each soul receives blessings for the new life to come.

The process of returning to earth can be very simple and direct.

We all go out onto a patio or portico, which is right at the edge of space and looks down at the earth. At first, I wonder why I would go back down there. I don't really want to return to earth, but my name is called and so I go. I jump over the edge and sort of slide down a moonbeam. I get smaller and change and finally become brand new again.

᭳

So I join my working group, and we look once again at the plan that we had made together. Now we get to the details, writing out the gene patterns and completing the scenarios and relationships. "Okay, I'll be there for you when you need it and you can help me out next time." We are making deals, and pumping each other up; "We can do it!" The entire group appears as young adults. I am a man; good-looking, sharp-featured, strong, and feeling powerful. On earth at this time, my great grandparents are alive, and soon the soul who will be my mother goes down a ray or shaft of light to be born.

᭳

It's time to be born. I'm standing on the edge and looking down. I see green trees and a river and mountains and fields, and then I dive off and glide down into a little house.

Spiritual Regressions: *Two Consecutive Incarnations Leading to the Present Life*

The next two journeys, which are successive lives just prior to the present incarnation, show the preparation over lifetimes that is necessary to awaken a soul to the varieties of the human predicament, and create capacities for deeper and more intensive consciousness and activities. This traveler, a young woman with a natural imaginative faculty, recounted both stories in the same session. The journey easily glided from one to the next.

Lifetime #1: *Young Male in the Southeastern United States in the Early 1900s*

I am being carried to a woman with long blonde hair, my mother. She is happy to see me. I am one year old and sitting on the ground in a meadow with my older brother and mother.

I have to go to school but I don't want to. But now I, Abraham, am being taken away from my mother. I'm only seven or so and they put me in a prison cell because I did something naughty. I stole something from the small town mayor's house at night, a key to a safe. Someone told me to do it—an older man. I was trying to make money for my mother and brothers, to keep food on the table. It's hard times. I'm wearing suspenders and knee pants. I'm just a little ragamuffin kid. And the officers are in suits. It's 1916. A thief is no good. They sit there for a long time.

Now I'm a bigger boy, sixteen years old and angry because I have been here in jail for a long time. They treat me like nothing, as though I don't exist, but at least they don't hit me or anything. When they let me out I run and run and run down the dirt roads because the prison is 'way out of town. No one is there to pick me up, so I walk on the roads for a long time. It's hot, flat, and dry, and there are no trees.

I'm in a large town now, trying to find my family. But where we lived before is all newly built, and there are funny automobiles, as well as rigs for transportation; and there are still horse-drawn coaches here, too. It's all new and big, and I don't know where to go. I need to get a job because I have no money. I go to a big white house to get a job from them. I am the stable-boy working with the horses. I have to learn because I don't know anything. There is a nice black man there. He takes care of the horses and we live over the barn. I am even learning to read and write.

I watch the pretty girls who live in the big house. I fall in love with one, and she falls in love with me, too. I'm in my early twenties; we are in love but we can't let anyone know, because I am the stable boy and she is the rich man's daughter. I get her pregnant: *not good*. She tries to abort the baby herself, and gets really ill. She is in her bed and I have to climb in her window to visit her in the night. She is ill and doesn't recognize me, and there is a big commotion because no one knows why she is ill. There is panic and commotion while I am there, because she begins to make noise. Someone is coming in, and I stand hidden behind the door.

I ask the black man about a witch doctor, and he arranges for someone to climb up with me. When the witch doctor sees my love, he says that she is going to die and nothing can be done. She jammed things up herself to abort herself, and she will die.

Now in her illness delirium, she is telling everything and babbling my name. The father is freaking out, and he is going to beat me with a rope. He is going to keep me in this room he has, and if his daughter dies, he will kill me too. I can only think about her and I am very upset. She dies, and I see the funeral through the window of the room I'm locked in, and I know her father is coming for me. He takes me into his study, pushing everyone away. The mother is screaming. He straps me to a mantle and stabs me with a big knife.

(Death) I only think of my love for the woman. I don't really feel anything. She is waiting for me on the other side. Her spirit is in the room, waiting for me. We are dematerializing through the walls and go upward. We are happy; there is lots of white light. We go off in our own separate ways, and that is okay. I'm going up into the light. I'm swooping around in white light/space, dancing around. There are other beings around but we are not in contact; everyone is doing their own thing.

(Reincarnation) I'm in a big mess hall, cafeteria-like place with lots of other souls, and we are all milling about. I was swooping around and the door is quite large; I didn't really mean to get caught in this pocket where you can't get out. There is a roof you can't go through once you get in; you can't get out like going through the walls on earth. I was wondering what this place was, so I swooped in and got caught; and now I see that you get let out only through the bottom. There are trapdoors in the floor; the ground gives way, and one at a time the beings here shoot down into the next life; but I don't think that we are really ready to do that yet.

The feelings are okay in this place, but the light here in this mess hall is darker than outside, where it is very brilliant. I didn't really make a choice to come here. It is an uneasy time and we all are talking about how we got here. Some were sent, and others like me just swooped in and got caught. Some beings are familiar, but there seem to be no major connections. It's quite full in here. You see someone you think you know and move toward them; although they are friendly, they are not the right one or who you thought they might be.

The larger grayish beings say that this is a holding tank for beings that need a different (special) experience. They need a specific lesson so they can learn to value life. This large gray one is a smart-ass. He says that if your last life was short, then the next one will be longer or harder so you can learn how to value human life.

The plans for the next life are allotted. The floor is full of drop-holes; when the one under you is opened, you go to where it takes you, most likely into a handicapped body. So if the last life was short and incomplete, then the next one will be long, or limited so that in the next one after that, you learn and experience the culmination of the last two lives. One learns to value life in a normal healthy human body.

I don't know if I'm ready to deal with the constraints that I might have to face in the next life; I really liked the body of the young virile man. I died at twenty, and was just getting into the power and physicality of the vibrant male body when my life was cut off. But it's the pattern and has to be that way.

At some point a beautiful other being from higher up is holding my face and radiating me and blessing me; then suddenly I go swish, down through the atmosphere of the earth into a tight, sloshy spot that is warm. I will be the handicapped boy. So I'm thinking, "Here goes." I'll give it my best shot, trusting that everything is going as it is supposed to. I know that it is okay. I enjoy the way down, turning and ready to accept my fate, because it's the only thing I can do. The crazy gray one spoke truth: I will go through the next constrained life, and then the next as M and keep on going.

Lifetime #2: *Handicapped Male in England or Scotland in the mid 1900s, and the Present Incarnation*

It was a pretty fast birth and I'm cold and shivering. I'm in a hospital, in a box thing. I don't think there is a mother; I don't feel her at all. Maybe she died. I'm not very observant or awake, maybe even handicapped. I am handicapped! I'm a boy with "Downs Syndrome" or something, in very sterile surroundings. Birth was very traumatic.

I'm growing up in an institution. A male person comes but it is all very blurry. There are cars, old and very rounded ones from the 1920s. I get to go outside. It's a nice sunny day and I am holding someone's hand and there is a big fence around the brick building. I feel happy, but there is only a small radius around me that I can perceive. We are walking, and then get into a car. I'm too little to see where we are going.

We are at a big house where some old person lives. I go in there. I'm sitting in a chair in an office and the older man is asking me questions. I don't answer. It's another place to live, with tall ceilings and big long halls. It's hard to get used to, it's so big; there are not many other people there, but it's nice. I can sit outside and I can work in the garden. I have no personal bonds in childhood and the teen years. There is just a nurse and the old man, and maybe a cook or something. When I'm twelve or so, there is someone ruffling my hair, but I don't notice faces or anything. The people are just there sort of helping me. I am handicapped and cannot see outside myself.

Someone is trying to teach me something, and I am angry and frustrated, running and screaming down the hallway. The old man catches me and holds me tight. It's the first time anyone really held me tight and hugged me. *(M. is crying here)* I put my head on his shoulder and cry and cry. He takes me by the hand and takes me to my room and sits with me till I fall asleep. He is being very loving. Life goes on. I am still living with the old man and I can perceive him more. There is a graduation and I am wearing a cap and gown and the old man watches from the audience, waving and smiling.

Someone else like me has come to the house. She is a handicapped girl who lives there now too. I feel good about it because we like each other. We hold hands and hug each other. We feel like children all the time, even though we must be older. I work in the garden. She swings on the swing. We wave to the old man. The girl and I are getting married; is this a game? Or real? She has a veil on and I hug her.

I am older now and ill. I don't know where the girl is. I'm in bed thrashing around and the nurses are coming. I don't talk much and I don't hear people speaking. I am being loud; they have to tie me down to the bed and they gave me a shot in my foot.

I'm old, not really years old, but I have aged now. I sit in a chair a lot and look out the window. There are children playing outside, but I'm tired and I sleep a lot in the chair and go slowly down the long hall to the eating place where it is quite loud and I sit alone at the long table. I take a tray to the very, very old man. He is very loving. I think I understand that he is going to die. He is patting my hand.

Yes, the old man died. There are many people there, and I walk behind the big brown casket. We walk through the town and back to the big house, and he is buried in the garden. I go there a lot and sit beside the grave.

I'm just in the house in my bed and I'm lying there. I don't want to do anything anymore. It is in the night and I get up and walk down the hall in the dark and I fall down the stairs and I'm lying on the floor. I rise out of the body and look at my body lying on the floor. Now I fly out the window, and I'm looking down on the house and garden, and everything down there. *(out of body experience)*

I thought I was dead, but now my body is sitting up again on the floor. Morning comes and someone helps me to bathe, but I'm not happy at all, just there. I am hitting my head on the wall; I want to die. I'm just sort of going crazy and it's not very fun. I decide to leave my body because I knew how to do it from my fall, which happened awhile ago.

(Death) I'm in bed and I just let go. I float down the hall and go out the same window that I went out when I fell, and I go up

into the night sky and keep on going. It's dark nighttime; I go up and break through a bubble surrounding the earth and into the light. It's very expansive; I can still feel the earth but I am getting farther away from it. I'm flying around, spinning and doing flips, and am happy. I land; it's all white light.

At some point there is a floor I can walk on, and light figures are forming and becoming clear and welcoming me. I am definitely one of these white light beings. I look like them. It's opening into green grass, a beautiful garden, lawns and beautiful trees. We lounge around and converse. We all communicate and simply understand that we are in the waiting area.

(Reincarnation) Here comes a reddish tinted being pointing at different ones, delegating them to a waiting line. I don't go to the waiting line, but I see that there is a dimensional door for the line to go through, but I continue to lounge around for a bit more. I'm lounging in my light-body thinking about that last handicapped lifetime, and not wanting to do that again. I learned the lesson. I do not want to be always a child and not perceiving life around me! My light-body wants a full human experience, and wants love in human form. The little bits of love I got from the old man were nice. So I want to experience love, family, and human connections in the next life.

Now, I am being pointed at by the larger pink-tinted being, and I get in line and go through the curtained doorway. It's like a night sky with stars and a slide you sit on and I slide down the slide into a watery place. The watery place is sloshy, and I can hear music and I'm in a new mom. I feel a walking or dancing movement; I can't see anything and it's dark, wet, and warm. I have memories of the garden. It was beautiful, peaceful, and rather short-lived. When I got on the slide, I knew my intention. I said, "I'm open for love and family and affection." I landed in a place where that was abundant, and I felt that right away. And now I'm getting born and I'm *me*.

Spiritual Regression: *A Woman in Ancient Greece and a simple Peasant Woman in Europe*

The following journey shows the results of exclusive attachment to one person during a lifetime. Although there is value in deep, intimate relationships, obsession or fixation on only one other person can have less-than-pleasant effects that must be resolved in kamaloca and succeeding lives. As individuals and as members of the family of humankind, we are social creatures and part of a larger community, which is the appropriate venue for our talents. The larger community is very much in need of our presence and energy. The traveler was profoundly moved by this session, and went on to resolve and integrate the issue in her present life.

I am standing on a cliff with rocks around, beside the sea. A wind is blowing, peaceful and free. I am a young woman with bare feet, and my sandals are set aside. I have long dark hair and am wearing a robe with embroidery on it. It is a pale yellowish-green. I came for a walk because someone I love will be going across the sea, so very far away. How can it be so beautiful right now? How can the shining sea be so beautiful, when he is going away? He will be gone soon. I just want it to stay like this (beautiful and complete), but I have to go home now.

There is no more peacefulness. He is getting ready to go, and I'm begging him not to. He takes me by the shoulders and says that he must go and that he will come home. It's a close bond, but I don't know if he is brother or lover. No, he is my brother, and I adore him and I'm afraid that he won't come back.

He is gone. It's a whole empty time going through the motions, doing chores, and so forth. I live with my mother only. The house is in the village by the sea, near Delphi. Many of the young men have gone to war. It's mostly women and children left. It's a very sad place right now.

Some of the ships come back with stories of war. He doesn't come. I keep looking for him, but he is not there. No one really saw him die or knows where he is. Though he promised to come back, he never comes. Life all goes by in a blur. There is someone else who asks to marry me, but I am not interested in anything. My mother dies. I miss her. Her heart was broken too. I bring in children from the village and teach the girls sewing and music, but it's all still very sad. It never stops being sad. I watch other friends with babies and husbands and children. I'm mostly around females this life.

(Death) When I die, I am not terribly old, but gray streaks my hair. I'm walking outside the village and have a sharp pain in my chest and fall down; it's my heart. My last thoughts are about my brother. Maybe I'll get to see him again and I'm not sad about going. I float free. I'm aware of the sea. I'm floating up above the shining sea. There is a lot of light. I'm looking for him but I don't see him. I see my mother; she smiles and reaches out. I just pass by. There is somebody way up ahead waiting who is very tall. I can't really see his face but he is very welcoming. I am confused and I ask about my brother. "Later," he says, "later." It's funny, but I feel young again. It is very beautiful here in the gardens, and I am walking across a stone-paved open courtyard between some buildings. I see a fountain. It's not that different from things I've known before. Some of the buildings look like temples. There are small groups of people walking or sitting.

I am with this first man who greeted me, and I have time to orient myself. This man is a teacher, father-like and very wise. Everywhere I look, I'm looking for my brother. The man says I won't be allowed to see him until I stop looking.

He leads me over to a group and says I'll be spending some time with them. These are other people who have "lost themselves" by giving themselves away to someone else. Our learning is to recognize that. We have to pull ourselves into our

165

own individual center. It is the energy-work of centering, and it feels strange and unfamiliar. We work in pairs, and I experience what it's like to allow my heart-energy to go out and get lost in my partner; then they walk away, and I feel empty. Then I work on being centered in my own heart so that I can flow out to the other person without losing my center; then when they walk away, I'm still here and full. There are other lessons about stages of soul development. Sometimes we have time to just walk and listen to music.

Now very gently we are moving outward from the center as we all go out on our individual journeys. I take up the thread from the last life, and it seems so small. I go into a hall to a meeting, and there is a table not quite in a U-shape. I stand in the open center and the council of five is at the table. They ask, "How will you carry this thread into the next life and what will you do with it?" I am accountable for describing this thread. The strength was in the love that I experienced. The weakness was in the immaturity and the lack of boundary. I got lost, and was not able to utilize that life beyond that point.

One of the council asks me about the particular individual (my brother) in the past life; if there is more to be completed. I am aware that it is more about the general lesson than about the individual; more about my losing myself than about who I lost myself to; but there is a karmic connection. When we meet again, there needs to be a completion, a coming together and moving apart, so that I can keep my own boundaries. It is more important that I keep focused on my own assignment to learn and serve. It is interesting to find out that after all the attachment and pining, it is not about him personally after all. I don't really have any interest in him. He was the means to the lesson. The last instructions from this council are, "Stay clear, and remember."

As I move on to a more specific place to plan the next incarnation, I see my brother on the way. We just exchange a greeting and acknowledgment; a passing, with a feeling of "more to come." In this new place, there is a being that I converse with; we discuss possibilities. I have a dual agenda: 1) To have a "practice run" around the ability to be connected and love, and yet to remain centered in the earthly journey. 2) To remember who I am in the next few lives; to remember my source, the mystery, the higher dimensional realities, and going home.

So I am trying to get a sense of what the choices are here. I see a life centered geographically in Europe, which would be simple, nothing exotic, just basic lessons. Then several consecutive lifetimes that will play out this theme.

I am remembering the original reason for becoming stuck here, which had to do with pride and arrogance; those had been from a number of past lives in Asia, and in one Celtic life. So there will be a series now of simple lives that are a counterbalance to the shadow of pride, thinking that I knew it all, and was independent and could do it on my own.

(Preparation for reincarnation) I am agreeing to be a female, to have a child-bearing life and to lose a child. There will be lessons around loving without losing my center, which is not always about losing a partner. In this life, it will be about losing a child and we have endless conversations on the theme.

The one who helps me in this planning reminds me that I have a tendency to impatience and that I should cultivate patience. Just before the descent into incarnation (it feels like surrender), I hear, "stay clear and remember."

Spiritual Regression: Observations of Contemporary Afterlife and State of the Spiritual Worlds in 2000

This final session included here (one of my own) is unique, in that the past life was not reviewed, because the connection with the spiritual guides was so direct and the perceptions of the afterlife were so clear. Members of my inner family naturally showed up to help and facilitate. We just jumped into spiritual observation and spiritual concepts, and flowed with each question that arose as a response to each spiritual visual or auditory experience.

(The induction into trance was primarily gentle relaxation, classic waves of warmth and a stairway leading down. At the bottom of the stairs, I simply lifted the veil and stepped behind it.)

There was my father who had died nine years before. He is happy, busy, and working with old friends like Ed, doing compassionate things such as helping other souls at the threshold who are traumatized when they enter the spiritual world. He has such a soft, loving heart, and he is planning the future good with Ed and others. He agreed to guide me into the spiritual worlds, and he offered to show me the overall pattern, the cosmic overview.

There is a threshold at the outer limit of the earth's atmosphere. The classic tunnel takes one from the surface of the earth, through the denseness, to the upper edge of the atmosphere where many beings (angels and discarnate people) are waiting to help, so the soul doesn't get stuck churning around. When the soul gets out of the tunnel and the earth's atmosphere, it is whisked away. So my father (we called him Gramps) and I are whisking through space.

Out beyond the earth's atmosphere, all space is filled with beings; it is not empty. We go to the temple between the earth and the moon (a circular walkway of two rows of pillars with a large hole in the middle for looking down on earth, which I call "the donut") and observe for a while from there. Souls are streaming up from the earth. Down close to the surface it is dense, dark, and agitated with all the souls who have died. Looking at the earth from this place near the moon, I see patches of light and dark. There is a lot of turmoil, but even in the darkest places, little beams of pink light shoot out high above. Actually, it looks like a mess.

Some souls are caught up in the churning, because of fear and unknowing. There are all kinds of snares for getting caught on earth and tricked into fear and anger, such as power (a big one), money, sex, greed, and hoarding possessions. I ask a trapped soul what it needs and it says, "We need to know what the fuck is going on." The dying need to know what is happening and what may happen! They need to know that they have inner eyes and ears, and to learn to open them.

Angels and other beings do come to earth in a supersensible vibrational space, but the souls that are angry and fearful don't see them, because they cannot vibrate at the same level as the angelic or discarnate human helpers. However, there will come a time when the caught, lost souls can be helped on the spiritual planes.

When Christ went down to the churning place in Hades after the crucifixion before Easter, He descended into hell, where He freed the souls of the dead that were caught and unable to continue their journey and incarnate again. And Christ said, "The works that I do, you can do likewise and even more." (John 14:12)

That is the thing to do. Every living human being can help by bringing light to the lost. Understanding and love are the light. There are helpers now, but in the future, there will be many more helpers of the souls of the dead. Perhaps in the farther future, someone will *always* help escort a newly released soul into the proper place. It will need to be done with guides, angels, and even Christ himself, who is the Lord of Karma. All need to have someone help them, someone who is known to them, some relative or friend.

I asked if I could go to help someone who is stuck, and it was okayed, so I went to R's family, because I know him. They are all "hung up" because they want to hoard and manipulate the family money. R, who is alive now, came with me in spirit. We approached the grandfather and got his attention, and I said, "Look up to Christ, He is the true Light. He will lift your burden of greed. He can make you free." The grandfather was willing to look at Christ and be lifted up. On the other hand, R's father snarled like an animal and was all hunched up over a pile of money. He was holding on with a death grip, so he could only gnash and bare his teeth to try to get us and Christ to go away. This was very hard on R, so Dorje (my Tibetan spiritual son) came to help him. Because Buddhism is the path that R has chosen to take at this time in his life, he responded to Dorje's offer of compassion and felt greatly relieved.

I saw and realized that the work with Hospice, and especially Compassion in Action, as well as other organizations working with the destitute who don't have anybody, and who could be so lost; are a tremendous service to their souls. I asked about war where the personal connection can be very slim. Gramps said, "If you pray for one soldier, it affects every one." There is a lot to do! As I was making the realizations about war, I went immediately to Vietnam because I know so many distressed souls who had traumatic experiences there, and I got stuck in Vietnam. *(The therapist pulled me back on track.)*

(Kamaloca—Moon Sphere) So then we whisked away to the moon which is a relay station. Here everyone sorts out according to their interests and beliefs, and they practice certain spiritual things. Some people are determined to create heaven and hell, right now! They are always erecting pearly gates so that they can walk through them.

The New Jerusalem is here, but is to be visited on the way back. It's over on the left. It is the beautiful ideal of how humanity could be. Now souls go on their forward journey to various places to see what they can bring back to it. By working diligently in the spirit world, souls can actually bring something of value and worth back to the moon sphere and place it in the New Jerusalem before they reincarnate again. They are adding to the possible evolution of humanity, by what each soul has discovered in the spiritual worlds between death and rebirth. It is offered as an addition or embellishment to the ideal and archetype of human existence, as symbolized and embodied in the New Jerusalem.

We first sort out when we reach the moon. The records of the Akashic Chronicle are available here. Most people find their extended family, and then wait in clusters until they are all assembled. Other than my father, who remains near the threshold because of his work, the rest of the family went on in little subgroups because it would be a long time for the whole cluster to close. Souls can move about in different clusters, but basically they have their family pods.

(Life Review) The groups go through their past lives together; they repent and ask forgiveness for the "bad" things, and celebrate the happy times. They don't have to do the life review alone. There are angelic beings that are helping; they don't interfere or change things, but "hand the souls a tissue," and that kind of help.

(Lower Devachan—Venus Sphere) When it is time to move on, the helpers bring the cluster to the next place. Here, in the Venus sphere, the souls congregate in larger groups according to the ability to love. It's like a love bath where being in the water brings to blossom whatever the soul has brought with it, like love, joy taken, and joy shared. If these are the love-qualities that the soul has experienced on earth, then the bath is nurturing, pleasurable, and enjoyed. The qualities that blossom in the bath are the qualities consciously expressed by the soul in life; the unconscious actions are neutral here. The real issue in life is in making good conscious choices, and then doing something about them!

Not far from us, some other souls are in a pretty cold bath, not nice, but awakening and difficult. People still have the opportunity to respond well or not. I am in a warm bath with a group and we invite the souls in the cold bath to come over and join us, and have the opportunity to try the warmth. But most of them feel the warm bath as scalding hot when they try to put a finger in to test the water. The warm love bath feels like a hot hell to most of them, so there are only two in this batch who want to make a change. The angels flock to them, rejoicing as they bring them over into the love. Some of the souls in the cold bath may decide to go back to earth at this time. One said, "At least there is some fun down there."

(Lower Devachan—Mercury Sphere) The next stage is a *big* opening as though the thousand-petalled lotus is blossoming, and real understanding comes with the opening. For instance, I saw the pattern of the cosmos and what the plan of existence might be. *(It was a comprehensive, flash experience for which I have yet to find words.)* Then the souls go on to the Sun. I lost track of Gramps here, but he had arranged the whole journey, so I went on.

(Sun Sphere—Transition) In the Sun there is a lot of rejoicing and excitement. Here people are making choices and planning for big journeys, big trips. Here in the Sun the individual is of prime importance; the clusters or groups do not function here. The Sun is the point of the divine cosmic intelligence and the original home of Christ. All is known in the Sun. The planets are different, individualized, specific modes of consciousnesses, but a complete being or ray of the whole divine Creator is shining right here in the Sun. It shines on all the planets, which are individual consciousnesses, different beings with different qualities. And it shines on people only half of the time.

When the soul enters the Sun sphere, it becomes as the Sun itself. Christ has always been in the Sun. He is the Solar Logos.

The Sun is a real ray of the Creator. Christ is a special ray of the Creator for Earth, in the fact that He came to earth and united all His conscious ego forces with earth and human destiny. When we reach the Sun, there is great rejoicing because a piece of Christ has returned to His home in the Sun. He is being made whole by human souls bringing Christed love and consciousness back to the Sun. It's like the story of Isis and Osiris: the story of the god being cut in pieces and being brought back together again.

Before the deed of Christ, it was different; and before the Fall, it was even differenter. Without the Fall in human evolution, it would have been like the warm pink baths, peaceful and co-operative with a very loving vibration, but no freedom. Since the Fall, from Lemuria to the time of Christ, what was the goal? The goal for humanity was to somehow hold the conscious connection with the Divine; because after the Fall, the connection with the Divine became more difficult to remember.

The early gods tried to help, although they would often use religion and humans for their own purposes. The whole system was slowly breaking down and wasn't working very well, until finally during Greek times, almost everyone at death was stuck in Hell and could hardly reincarnate. Humanity was diseased physically and etherically. Evolution wasn't going forward any more.

It took the deed of Christ to turn human devolution around. Always, throughout time, there was a knowing that the Christ would come. The savior from the Sun was foretold in most religions. The god who would heal all humanity through his death and resurrection was prophesized all over the world. Zoroaster referred to Ahura Mazda; Apollo, was the Greek Sun God with origins in the Hyperboreans of antiquity; those were ancient times, even for the Greeks.

The Sun will be a Super Nova, but we have a ways to go before then. That will be the point when everyone is at the vibration of the Sun, and humans will live at that level. We will all go together when we go.

(Higher Devachan) When the choices and plans are all made and the soul is ready, it is almost like one is "spit out"; the soul is propelled out of the Sun and flies toward its destination.

(Higher Devachan—Mars, Jupiter, and Saturn Spheres) As the soul flies, it goes through the orbits of the planets which are living forces. The reason the planet is in the particular orbit is because that area of the universe is a specific vibration which is in harmony with the energy of the planet's consciousness. So the soul moves out through the orbits and experiences sound, color, depths, and other sensations which have no name.

(Into the Stars toward the Midnight Hour of Existence) You travel out to where you are going, to some star or another galaxy, but I think you stay within this universe. After leaving our solar system, the soul is beyond the Christ influence, into another place, with other languages, other laws, and "other everythings." I sped out through the zodiac and into "space" to another planet with other colors, toward the purple and lavender spectrum, with a viscous atmosphere. The beings do not really incarnate physically, but are more like dense auras. It is a nice, nice place, because they all chose to make this a nice place and they co-operate.

From an open point of view out high above another planet, I am watching how another world chooses to be; what another completely different existence is. The people or beings are pink, furry, or ciliated, with many appendages. The feeling is warm, lovely, co-operative, sympathetic, and compassionate. I dive down among them and snuggle into a divine experience. Every sense is drenched in love. I dissolve in rosey joy. When I finally extricate myself and rise up to leave, I receive a gift, a remembrance, a little piece of pink ciliated love so that I can remember that state and live in it.

The worlds that have become so mechanistic are the ones on the downside (hung up in materiality and too physical); they have to do with being afraid to die and transform. But even the negative worlds are just a phase, a passing phase. I see the difficulty in creating machines to replace human beings; machines don't have a soul and are out of place in the whole cosmic design. The pattern of evolution throughout this universe is based on multiple levels, and on the transformation of the lower, denser vibrations into higher, finer energies. Without a soul, the machines cannot evolve and transform; they are static. What we project our potential into, such as computers and machines, we as humans need to learn to do ourselves. All our dormant DNA is waiting to be activated rather than to have the possibilities projected out of ourselves and into machines. We could lose the ability to manifest latent powers by not using them and becoming dependent on computers and machines to do the difficult things for us. Other worlds are like the Dark Ages, very dense and brutal. I wouldn't want to go there and didn't.

Star Wars is real. Various worlds are doing a lot of different things; unfortunately, some of the violent ones are on the move.

(Return to the Sun Sphere) Returning to the Sun on the way back to the moon and earth, is almost like going through a cash register; the soul receives a reward, something of value, a little golden disk with slots and indentations and symbols on it, and it shines and glows. This has the information that the soul learned from having journeyed to other places. It's like a record of your journey and a template or pattern for the kind of incarnation you can have next time.

(Return to the Moon Sphere) Back on the moon, Gramps was waiting for me. The little golden "punch card" from the Sun, tells what kind of a life you can fit into on earth. As souls wait in the moon sphere, the destiny on the little golden thing shows the proper genetic makeup of the future mother and father.

Everyone gets a tour of the New Jerusalem before going back, as a reminder of the possibility of heaven on Earth; what Earth could be, and what it will be like in the far future. As souls go through the New Jerusalem, they leave the gifts from the star worlds that they visited and observed during the long journey out into the galaxies. That way, new impulses and ideas become incorporated into the future vision of humanity and of the earth. So I leave my little piece of pink love there. But I always remember that feeling because it was imprinted on my golden disc and imprinted in my genetic makeup. Now, in this life, because the earth is dark, and is painful with lots of heavy karma attached, the heroism of love in the face of all the insanity is my story and part of my destiny. *("Kurkurbita." I simply heard this word clearly enunciated.)*

(Moon School) There are lots of different realms/places/ schools in the moon sphere.

It is difficult to say much about the intellectual philosophies and religions that believe that the soul just goes into nirvana. They create that nirvana space in the moon, but then, the human souls with those beliefs don't have the whole afterlife experience. They stay in the moon for a long time, because it is just the personal mind. They go to the self-created zendo for a long time. When they finally walk out, they have choices, because it is different from what they thought. Sometimes they choose to incarnate again; some choose to go on the after-death journey. It just takes them a really long time. Or they may choose to join a group. That's the usual way. Most intellectual people get caught up into their like-minded group, which remains static in their belief system. Some groups have made decisions about how to come back; they make a plan, like the Buddhists. Some of the more spiritual Buddhists meditate more deeply and find themselves in Dorje's school to learn other ways of doing the after-death journey. There are many options.

Atheists are often stuck close to the earth because they don't have a spiritual frequency developed within themselves. Many don't even get up to the moon. They stay stuck in the etheric realms, although they may get to the moon through the help of friends and other beings. They may go to a place of "nothing" because that is what they believe. They can move if they want to, but they usually don't know that it is their desire and belief that has created their experience, and don't know that they have a choice. The experiences after death are a more dramatic presentation or manifestation of how we create our life here on earth. These states of mind become the reality on the moon. We personally create our own heaven, hell, nirvana or other after-death experience through our thoughts and beliefs from life.

All those who died in concentration camps (and I am one) went to a special place. It was a warm, bland space in which healing could happen, because life and death had been so violent and the souls were in shock. Death by cyanide (as happened in the holocaust) damages the etheric body as well as the physical, and so the journey is cut short. Souls who die by cyanide or atomic annihilation can choose to stay a shorter or longer time in the healing place; but those who have had their etheric bodies damaged or destroyed get no farther than the moon. We all came back into earth life very quickly because of the manner of our death.

The practices of Tibetan Buddhism encourage living with death, in a way, or living in both worlds, through visualizations. It's like living death; but then life may not be what it could be, if it is hindered by the constancy of death images. Finding a balance is crucial. I asked Dorje, "What's important here?" The answer, "It is important that Buddhism be expanded so that more and greater development can happen in the spiritual worlds after death."

In the Hindu and Egyptian religions of the far, far past, many of the gods were part animal, or were other than human. These gods, or beings from other systems, had their whole religious programs for life and also for death; so that when people died who were followers of their way, the souls went into those god's specific areas of the spiritual world. The pattern was totally different in those ancient days. The souls learned their lessons from the gods after death. First they learned just one particular lesson from one god, and later they all played a part.

It was the coming of Christ that brought divine, godly qualities right down into the bodies, hearts, and minds of human beings. This set a new pattern in the genetic makeup of humankind, including Christ-consciousness and the possibility of consciousness throughout both life and death.

Christ and Rudolf Steiner both say it is very important that humanity understand the full cycles of sleeping and waking, death and rebirth. People need to experience both life and death consciously. Before the deeds of Christ, death was painful and hard, and it was impossible to remain conscious throughout. Now everyone has the opportunity to become aware and remain conscious; to learn the lessons clearly for themselves; and to consciously evolve. But unfortunately, most people sleep right through it. We need cooperation between the living and the dead and among all of us, to accomplish Lucid Death. And we need it now!

"THAT'S ALL FOR NOW, FOLKS," said a funny little voice.

Summary and Conclusion

It is universally acknowledged that at death, something leaves the body. The body then begins to return to its constituent earthly elements and ultimately ceases to exist as a body. Beyond that single fact which is physically observable and scientifically quantifiable, there is no further consensus. Who or what is that unseen something that transcends, and what happens to it when it leaves the body?

The world's religions have addressed this issue (the soul, whither and whence) in diverse ways; and the beliefs have changed and adapted through the ages and around the globe. Religious dogma spans views as diverse as complete annihilation of the soul on one hand, or eternal heaven or hell on the other hand; instantaneous reincarnation into objects in nature, or a process spanning days or centuries; physical resurrection or spiritual existence as light and color. Some religions describe after-death environments; others do not.

Many people, from times long past to the present, have had experiences beyond the threshold of death in the spiritual worlds, and lived to tell about them. Phenomena such as the near-death experience, vision quests, dreams, and meditation have afforded glimpses of non-physical dimensions. Multiple complex landscapes can be extrapolated from the wealth of information concerning the possible afterlives; information accumulated throughout the eons of human history.

Although vast, contradictory, and confusing, it is possible to organize and comprehend the disparate information when a philosophical basis is laid that includes the nature of humankind and the evolution of consciousness in the physical and spiritual worlds. Within that framework, the various and changing dogmas can be seen as beliefs metamorphosed through the pressures of expanding consciousness over time, as humanity has penetrated more and more deeply into understanding the material world; and as mystics of all times and cultures have ascended into spiritual realms.

The esoteric western tradition contains ancient wisdom that has been interpreted and renewed periodically by highly initiated individuals. In the nineteenth and twentieth centuries, a resurgence of interest resulted in the founding of the Theosophical Society and the modern Rosicrucian Orders. Rudolf Steiner, through his "spiritual scientific" approach to phenomena, developed the body of work called Anthroposophy. The ancient hidden wisdom is now public, and accessible to any open-minded, clear-thinking person. A conceptual framework for understanding the reasons and modus operandi of the cosmic patterns of life and death is useful for understanding the necessity of death and its eventual overcoming. There is meaning and value in all existence: both life and death.

The concept that humanity's constitution consists of physical, etheric, astral, and spiritual components (each of which have developed over eons of time, and been described and expressed in different ways throughout the ages), creates a sufficiently broad basis for understanding life and the life after death. The physical and etheric bodies are the ground of the will, the instrument for action. The astral body encompasses the emotions, and the spiritual aspect of a human being is the Ego/I which is the self-conscious individuality capable of conceptualization, thought, and ultimately, of spiritual perception.

During life on earth, a human being garners a wide variety of physical, emotional, and mental experiences through these four bodies. The experiences offer lessons and learning that are processed to a greater or lesser degree during the lifetime. What is left unfinished, as well as the accumulated wisdom, are brought into the spiritual world at death. That which is carried beyond death is known as individual karma or personal responsibility. These karmic residues are processed and resolved after death, so that the experiences of one lifetime are transformed into faculties and capacities for the next life.

As in life, there are four general categories of completion in death: the physical, the etheric, the astral, and the spiritual. The first is accomplished in leaving the physical body to the laws of the material world. The second is the dissolution of the etheric body into the ether of the planet. The etheric dissolution releases a life-review, which is impressed on the astral body, and which many people who have had a near-death experience have observed. The resolution of the astral body takes place in kamaloca, the moon sphere. In kamaloca, which is similar to the Christian purgatory, all emotional experiences are resolved. One receives and feels everything that one has done or perpetrated on others in life. In this way, one experiences a heaven or hell of one's own making. When the emotional processes have been completed, the Ego/I alone, moves on.

The resolution of the many aspects of the thinking consciousness and spirit realities takes place within the planetary spheres. The inner planets, Venus and Mercury, make up the realm called Lower Devachan. In each planet, the Ego/I resolves specific qualities: Venus, love; and Mercury, intellect. The Sun is the turning point from personal karma that is completed here because it applies to our solar system, to cosmic consciousness, as the essence of the individuality moves out into Higher Devachan through Mars, Jupiter, and Saturn, and the distant planets.

Ultimately, when the spiritualized Ego/I is free of all earthly attachments, it moves out through the zodiac to the midnight hour of existence in Galactic Center before returning to earth with renewed and evolved abilities for the next incarnation, gathered as the individual essence returns through the planets. In each planetary sphere, the Ego/I of the new incarnation begins to acquire new capacities, faculties, and talents that have been metamorphosed from the past. After waiting in the moon sphere till the astrological conditions are right, the new Ego/I with its germinal astral body from the moon, gathers etheric forces from the etheric body of the earth as it descends to reincarnate in the fetus in the mother's body and the circle is complete.

The Tibetan Buddhist cosmology is somewhat similar to the western esoteric paradigm, although it is described in very different cultural images. The cycle of human life is experienced as a series of four bardos (transitional states). When the Bardo of Life has come to its appointed end, the individual enters the Painful Bardo of Dying. If the expiring soul does not achieve enlightenment at the first dawning of the clear light and remain within it, then the soul is destined to travel through the Luminous Bardo of Dharmata, which is a journey into the realms of the Deities and their consorts, both benign and wrathful. If enlightenment or transcendence of attachment has not yet been achieved during this bardo, the soul then enters the Bardo of Becoming and reincarnation, and once again, the cycle is completed as life begins anew.

Life gives us the experiences that undergo evolutionary transformation in death. Through death, the human spirit is equipped with evolved faculties for another life. The spirit spirals ever higher through life and death and into life again in infinitely expanding consciousness. Ultimately, we will remain aware through all facets of existence. At the present time, death is still necessary because consciousness has not penetrated into the deepest heart of matter, or resolved all earthly actions. As evolution and consciousness expand to embrace all knowledge and feeling, all subconscious impulses, and all former lives and relationships, we as individuals change; and the world changes, too. As we heal and make amends, finally penetrating every activity with the light of compassionate consciousness, death need not be.

The veils between the worlds are becoming thin; even quantum physics is proclaiming the interchangeability of matter and energy. Perhaps it is time now to invite the quantum leap into our personal lives and acknowledge our own angels and imps, our connections with supersensible realms; and time to admit that death is simply a journey into those realms which surround us unseen in life. Common sense says that any long journey to a foreign land deserves preparation. So, should we choose to accept death as a journey into supersensible lands (lands that sympathetically vibrate with our thinking and feeling, rather than with our bodies), we might indeed prepare for and experience *Lucid Death: Conscious Journeys Beyond the Threshold,* and step boldly into our adventures in Death's domain.

Biography

Kienda Betrue, IMA (Independent Master of Art) in Thanatology, Antioch University and Clinical Hypnotherapist.

Since childhood, I have wanted to know why I was born and why I am living. And if there is purpose to my life, then why and what is death, and what in heaven's (or hell's) name happens when I die? The SIDS (Sudden Infant Death Syndrome) death of my son, Christian Alexander, intensified my desire to understand, so I studied death and the journey beyond. With Christian's help from the spiritual world, I found that it is possible to know what lies beyond the threshold, and after many experiences over time, I am familiar and comfortable with Death.

Although there is a wealth of anecdotal information from the many near-death experiences, and from traditional religious beliefs, nowhere did I find a context or philosophy comprehensive enough to contain and integrate all the information. Finally, the western esoteric traditions of Anthroposophy and Rosicrucianism presented a matrix vast enough to organize all the pieces. After years of personal exploration and academic research, I am delighted to have synthesized an understanding of why I was born, am living, and will die, and what happens after.

In 1992, I created Syntheself, a hypnotherapy counseling practice and have facilitated spiritual regression sessions in the United States, Austria, England, Germany, and India. I specialize in journeys that further conscious evolution, such as past lives and after-death experiences, soul care, and journeys into archetypal realms; integrating all aspects for balance, harmony, wholeness, and courage to face the future.

I bring extensive experience through my own life path which has included: Reiki Master, Institute of Cultural Affairs Facilitation Training, Interdimensional Consciousness Training. Minister of Spiritual Healers and Earth Stewards (SHES), Multi-dimensional Cellular Healing, SIDS Grief Counselor, Hospice, Tai Chi Chuan, Firewalking, Omega, Tarot, Subud, Sufi Healing Order, International Association of Near-Death Studies (IANDS), Emotional Freedom Techniques (EFT), Rites of Passage, Costume Design, Theater Production, Singing, Motherhood, Waldorf Education, and Anthroposophy.

Lucid Death: Conscious Journeys Beyond the Threshold is my first book. A number of others are in process already—*Aberrations in Heaven and Hell: When Life Impinges Upon Death, The Dragon Quartet: A History of Dragon Evolution in the Universe, Tulku Tales from India: Changing Patterns of Reincarnation, The Devolution of Evil: from the Julio-Claudian Emperors to the Third Reich,* and *R & S & I.*

I offer workshops also—*The Good News About Death: Adventures in Death's Domain, Reincarnation and Karma: How Does It Really Work?* and *A Conceptual Matrix of the Cosmos: Humanity's Place in Time and Space.*

Kienda can be reached at www.lucid-death.com

ENDNOTES

1. Pfeiffer, Ehrenfried. *The Heart Lectures.* Spring Valley, NY: Mercury Press, 1982, p. 4.

2. Steiner, Rudolf. *Cosmic Memory: Prehistory of Earth and Man.* Englewood, NJ: Rudolf Steiner Publications, Inc., 1959, p. 107.

3. Steiner, Rudolf. *Theosophy of the Rosicrucian.* London: Rudolf Steiner Press, 1981, p. 107.

4. Steiner, Rudolf. *Life Between Death and Rebirth.* Spring Valley, NY: Anthroposophic Press, Inc., 1968, p. 8.

5. Steiner, Rudolf. *The Evolution of Consciousness.* Letchworth, England: The Garden City Press Limited, 1926, p. 155.

6. Reproduced by kind permission of Floris Books, Edinburgh, from *Though You Die: Death and Life Beyond Death* by Stanley Drake © The Christian Community 1962, 2002, p. 53.

7. Op. cit., Steiner, Rudolf. *Life Between Death and Rebirth*, pp. 250-251.

8. Op. cit., Drake, Stanley.

9. Ibid., pp. 54-55.

10. Ibid., pp. 55-56.

11. Op. cit., Steiner, Rudolf. *The Evolution of Consciousness*, pp. 161-162.

BIBLIOGRAPHY

The most salient books are starred (*), and the books from which direct quotes of any length are taken, are double starred (**). The translations of the *Bardo Thodrol (The Tibetan Book of the Dead)* that are the basis of Chapter 5—Buddhism, are marked with a pound sign (#).

*Archiati, Pietro. *Reincarnation in Modern Life*. London: Temple Press, 1997.

*Atwater, P.M.H. and David H. Morgan. *The Complete Idiot's Guide to Near-Death Experiences*. Indianapolis, IN: alpha books, 2002.

Baker, Linda. *Soul Contracts*. Kearney, NE: Patchwork Press, 1998.

*Beckh, Herman. *From Buddha to Christ*. Edinburgh, England: Floris Books, 1925.

Chagdud Tulku Rinpoche. *Life in Relation to Death*. Junction City, CA: Padma Publishing, 1987.

*Coward, Howard (ed.). *Life after Death in World Religions*. Maryknoll, NY: Orbis Books, 1999.

*Debusschere, Evelynn B. *The Revelation of Evolutionary Events in Myths, Stories and Legends*. Fair Oaks, CA: The Association of Waldorf Schools of North America, 1997.

*Delog Dawa Drollma. *Delog: Journey to Realms Beyond Death*. Junction City, CA: Padma Publishing, 1995.

Deverell, Doré. *Light Beyond the Darkness: The Healing of a Suicide Across the Threshold of Death*. London: Temple Lodge Publishing, 1996.

Dossey, Larry. *Reinventing Medicine – Beyond Mind-Body to the New Era of Healing*. NewYork: HarperSanFrancisco, 1999.

**Drake, Stanley. *Though You Die: Death and Life Beyond Death*. London: The Christian Community Press, 1962. Edinburgh: Floris Books, 2002.

#Freemantle, Francesca and Chogyam Trungpa. *The Tibetan Book of the Dead*. Boston and London: Shambhala, 1975.

*Frieling, Rudolf. *Christianity and Reincarnation*. Edinburgh: Floris books, 1977.

Glas, Norbert, M.D. *The Fulfillment of Old Age*. Hudson, NY: Anthroposophic Press, Inc., 1970.

*Grof, Stanislav and Christina Grof. *Beyond Death: The Gates of Consciousness*. London: Thames and Hudson, 1980.

Grof, Stanislav and Joan Halifax. *The Human Encounter with Death*. London: Souvenir Press, (E & A) Ltd., 1977.

Groves, Richard F. and Mary L. Groves. *The Sacred Art of Dying – Unit 1, Diagnosing and Addressing Spiritual Pain*. Bend, OR: The Sacred Art of Living Center, 2000.

Hancock, Graham. *Finger-Prints of the Gods*. New York: Three Rivers Press, 1992.

**Head, Joseph, and S.L. Cranston (eds.). *Reincarnation: An East-West Anthology*. Wheaton, IL: The Theosophical Publishing House, 1961.

**Heindel, Max. *The Rosicrucian CosmoConception*. Hammond, IN: W.B. Conkey Company, 1937.

*Irish, Donald P., Kathleen F. Lindquist, and Vivian Jenkins Nelsen. *Ethnic Variation in Dying, Death, and Grief*. Washington, DC: Taylor & Francis, 1993.

Jaynes, Julian. *The Origin of Consciousness in the Breakdown of the Bicameral Mind*. Boston: Houghton Mifflin Company, 1976.

*Jung, Carl G. *Memories, Dreams, and Reflections*. New York: Vintage Books, Random House, 1965.

Kenyon, Tom. *Brain States*. Naples, FL: United States Publishing, 1994.

*Kramer, Kenneth. *The Sacred Art of Dying: How World Religions Understand Death*. Mahwah, NJ: Paulist Press, 1998.

Kolisko, Eugene. *The Human Organism in the Light of Anthroposophy*. Bournemouth, England: Kolisko Archive Publications, 1978.

Kubler-Ross, Elizabeth. *On Life After Death*. Berkeley: Celestial Arts, 1991.

LaBerge, Stephen and Howard Reingold. *Exploring the World of Lucid Dreaming*. New York: Ballantine Books, 1990.

#Lati, Rinpoche and Jeffrey Hopkins. *Death, Intermediate States, and Rebirth*. Ithaca: Snow Lion Publications, Inc., 1997.

*Miller, Sukie. *After Death: How People Around the World Map the Journey After Life*. New York: A Touchstone Book by Simon & Schuster, 1997.

**Mishlove, Jeffrey. *Coming into Being: Artifacts and Texts in the Evolution of Consciousness*. New York: A Random House Booksworks Book, 1975.

Montgomery, Ruth. *A World Beyond*. New York: Fawcet, 1971.

Moody, Raymond A. Jr. *Life After Life*. New York: Bantam Books, 1975.

Morse, Melvin. *Closer to the Light: Learning from the Near-Death Experiences of Children*. New York: Ivy Books, 1990.

Mullin, Glenn H. *Living in the Face of Death: The Tibetan Tradition*. Ithaca: Snow Lion Publications, 1998.

*Newton, Michael. *Destiny of Souls: New Case Studies of Life Between Lives*. St. Paul, MI: Llewellyn Publications, 2000.

**Pfeiffer, Ehrenfried. *The Heart Lectures*. Spring Valley, NY: Mercury Press, 1982.

*Ring, Kenneth. *Lessons from the Light – What We Can Learn From the Near-Death Experience*. Portsmouth, NH: Moment Point Press, 1998.

Ritchie, George G. and Elizabeth Sherrill. *Return From Tomorrow*. Grand Rapids, MI: Fleming H. Revell, 1978.

Roszell, Calvert. *The Near-Death Experience*. Hudson, NY: The Anthroposophic Press, 1992.

Schneider, Meriam and Jan Selliden Bernard. *Midwives to the Dying*. Sherwood, OR: Angel's Work, 1992.

Sharp, Kimberly Clark. *After the Light: The Spiritual Path to Purpose*. New York: Avon Books, 1996.

*Singh, Kathleen Dowling. *The Grace in Dying – How We Are Transformed Spiritually As We Die*. New York: HarperSanFrancisco, 1998.

**Smith, Houston. *The Illustrated World Religions: A Guide to our Wisdom Traditions*. San Francisco: HarperSanFrancisco, HarperCollins Publishers, 1994.

#Sogyal Rinpoche. *The Tibetan Book of Living and Dying*. San Francisco: HarperSanFrancisco, HarperCollins Publishers, 1994.

Steiner, Rudolf. *The Bridge Between Universal Spirituality and the Physical Constitution of Man*. Spring Valley, NY: The Anthroposophic Press, 1958.

**Steiner, Rudolf. *Cosmic Memory: Prehistory of Earth and Man*. Englewood, NJ: Rudolf Steiner Publications, Inc., 1959.

**Steiner, Rudolf. *The Evolution of Consciousness*. Letchworth, England: The Garden City Press Limited, 1926.

*Steiner, Rudolf. *Knowledge of Higher Worlds and its Attainment*. Spring Valley, NY: Anthroposophic Press, Inc., 1947.

**Steiner, Rudolf. *Life Between Death and Rebirth*. Spring Valley, NY: Anthroposophic Press, Inc., 1968.

Steiner, Rudolf. *An Occult Physiology*. London: Rudolf Steiner Press, 1951.

*Steiner, Rudolf. *An Outline of Occult Science*. Spring Valley, NY: Anthroposophic Press, Inc., 1972.

Steiner, Rudolf. *Reincarnation and Karma*. North Vancouver, Canada: Steiner Book Centre, Inc., 1977.

*Steiner, Rudolf. *Theosophy*. New York: Anthroposophic Press, Inc., 1971.

**Steiner, Rudolf. *Theosophy of the Rosicrucian*. London: Rudolf Steiner Press, 1981.

Tart, Charles T. *Body, Mind, Spirit: Exploring the Parapsychology of Spirituality*. Charlottesville, VA: Hampton Roads Publishing Co., Inc., 1997.

Tenzin Wangyal Rinpoche. *The Tibetan Yogas of Dreams and Sleep*. Ithaca: Snow Lion Publications, 1998.

#Thurman, Robert A.F. *The Tibetan Book of the Dead*. New York: Bantam Books, 1994.

*Wachsmuth, Guenther. *The Evolution of Mankind*. Dornach, Switzerland: Philosophic-Anthroposophic Press, 1961.

*Weiss, Brian L. *Many Lives, Many Masters*. New York: A Fireside Book Published by Simon & Schuster, 1988.

What Dreams May Come. Dir. Vincent Ward. Screenplay by Ronald Brass. Perf: Robin Williams, Cuba Gooding Jr., Annabella Sciorra. Universal, 1998.

Wilbur, Ken. *The Spectrum of Consciousness*. Wheaton, IL: Quest Books, The Theosophical Publishing House, 1997.

Wilson, Ian. *The After Death Experience: The Physics of the Non-Physical*. New York: William Morrow and Company, Inc., 1987.

Zaleski, Carol. *Otherworld Journeys: Accounts of Near-Death Experiences in Medieval and Modern Times*. New York: Oxford University Press, 1987.